R  f

- Descriptions in this r Samsung Galaxy S9/S9 Plus.

- All information supplied in this guide is for educational purpose only, and users bear the responsibility for using it.

- All information supplied in this guide was what was available as at the time of writing this guide, and it may not be 100% accurate again if there is a major firmware/software update to Samsung Galaxy S9/S9 Plus.

- Depending on your local network service provider or your location/region, some of the features discussed in this guide may not be available on your Samsung Galaxy S9/S9 Plus.

- Although I took tremendous effort to ensure that all pieces of information provided in this guide are correct, I will welcome your suggestions if you find out that any information provided in this guide is inadequate or you find a better way of doing some of the actions mentioned in this guide. All correspondences should be sent to pharmibrahimguides@gmail.com

About This Guide

Finally, a simplified guide on Samsung Galaxy S9/S9 Plus is here– this guide is indeed a splendid companion for these two high-end phones.

This is a very thorough, no-nonsense guide, useful for both experts and newbies. This guide contains a lot of information on Samsung Galaxy S9/S9 Plus.

It is full of actionable steps, hints, notes, screenshots and suggestions. This guide is particularly useful for newbies/beginners and seniors; nevertheless, I strongly believe that even the techy guys will find some benefits reading it.

Enjoy yourself as you go through this very comprehensive guide.

PS: Please make sure you do not give the gift of Samsung Galaxy S9/S9 Plus without giving this companion guide alongside with it. This guide makes your gift a complete one.

Table of Contents

How to Use This Guide (Please Read!)

This guide is an unofficial manual of Samsung Galaxy S9/S9 Plus and it should be used just like you use any reference book or manual.

To quickly find a topic, please use the table of contents. This would allow you to quickly find information and save time.

When I say you should carry out a set of tasks, for example, when I say you should tap **Settings > Sound > Notifications & actions**, what I mean is that you should tap on **Settings** and then tap on **Sound**. And lastly, you should tap on **Notifications & actions**. When a function is enabled or turned on, the status switch will appear bold and colored. On the other hand, when a function is disabled or turned off, the status switch will appear gray.

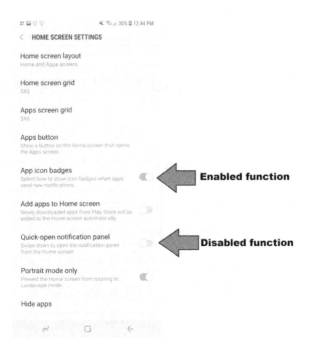

I hope this guide helps you get the most out of your smartphone.

Getting Started with Your Phone

Unpacking Your Device

It is quite easy to unbox your Samsung Galaxy S9/S9 Plus. Just use your hand to press the inner box so that it sticks out. Then use a knife to cut the seal (if any) and carefully open the box.

When you unpack your product box, check your product box for the following items:

1. Samsung Galaxy S9/S9 Plus
2. USB charging cable & power adapter
3. Quick Reference Guide
4. Earphones
5. USB connector (USB Type-C)
6. Eject Pin (the eject pin is located on the case that house the "quick start guide")
7. Micro USB Connector

Hint: I will advise that you are careful when removing the eject pin from the case (the eject pin is located on the case that houses the "quick reference guide") so as not to prick your hand in the process.

Turning Your Phone on/off and Setting Up Your Phone

Just like many other smartphones, turning on your device is as simple as ABC. To turn on your phone, press and hold the Power Key until you notice a small vibration. If you are turning on your phone for the first time, please carefully follow the on-screen instructions to set it up. You will have the option to connect to a Wireless network during the setup, to learn more about connecting your phone to Wi-Fi, please go to page 316. In addition, I will advise that you insert the SIM Card before switching on your phone. To learn more about inserting the SIM card, please go to page 25.

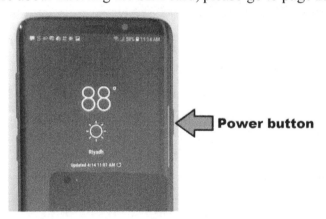 **Power button**

To turn off your phone, press and hold the power key and select **Power off.** Select **Power off** again to confirm.

Hint: If you don't feel like switching off your phone again and you want to dismiss the power off screen, simply tap the back button. Alternatively, tap anywhere outside the onscreen icons.

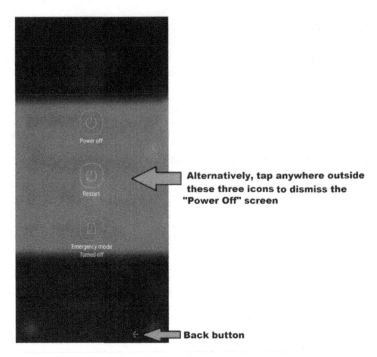

Alternatively, tap anywhere outside these three icons to dismiss the "Power Off" screen

Back button

In addition, if you are using the phone for the first time, remove any protective nylon from the surface of the phone.

Please do not vex if you find it unnecessary reading about how to on/off your device. I have included it, in case there may be someone reading this guide who is a complete novice and knows close to nothing about smartphones.

Tips:

- Some network provider may require you to enter a PIN when you switch on your phone. You can try entering **0000.** This is the default PIN for many network providers. If you have problem entering the correct PIN, please contact your network service provider.

- During the setup, you may skip a process by tapping **SKIP** located at the bottom of the screen. Usually, you will have the option to perform this process in the future by going to your phone settings.

- While using your phone for the first time, you may have the option to transfer your contents from your old phone to Samsung Galaxy S9/S9 Plus. Just carefully follow the onscreen instructions to do this. If you skip the process of content transfer during the phone setup, and you will like to perform the transfer now, please see page 42 to learn how to go about this.

- Because of software updates and installations, it is likely that Samsung Galaxy S9/S9 Plus will consume a large amount of data during the setup, I will advise that you connect to a wireless network if you can. Using a mobile network during the setup may be expensive.

- When you start using Samsung Galaxy S9/S9 Plus, you may probably notice that its screen locks within few seconds after you finish interacting with it. To allow the screen stay longer before it locks, change the screen timeout setting. To do this:

  o Swipe down from the top of the screen and select

  Settings icon ⚙ .

  o Tap **Display**.

  o Scroll down and tap on **Screen Timeout**. Then choose an option.

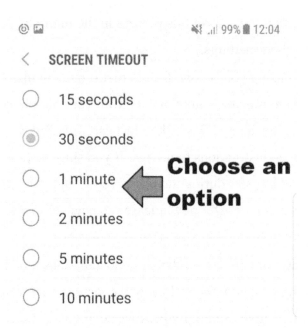

Please note that selecting a longer timeout may make your battery discharge faster.

- *Do you need to charge your phone before first use?*
  To the best of my knowledge, it is not necessary. If you charge it before first use, that is cool, but if there is no way to charge it, then you can use it straightaway without charging it. I have learnt that the new lithium batteries used in smartphones don't really need to be charged before first use (provided that the battery still has power).

Get to Know Your Device

Device Layout

Please note that Samsung Galaxy S9 and Samsung Galaxy S9 Plus look very similar except few differences. In the picture shown below, I have used Samsung Galaxy S9 Plus as an example.

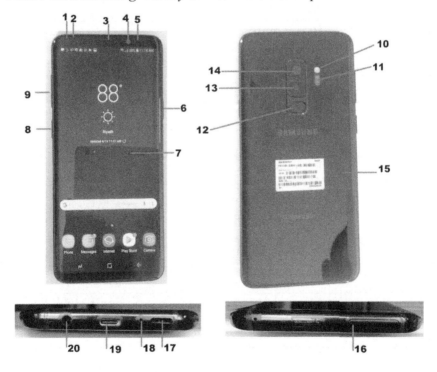

Number	Function
1.	LED indicator. This gives different colors depending on what is happening on the phone.
2.	Proximity sensors
3.	Receiver/Earpiece
4.	Front camera
5.	Iris Scanner
6.	Power button
7.	Touch Screen
8.	Bixby button
9.	Volume up and down button
10.	Flash
11.	Heart Rate sensor
12.	Fingerprint Sensor
13.	Rear camera
14.	Rear camera
15.	Back side of the phone
16.	SIM and Memory Card Tray
17.	Speaker
18.	Microphone. Please ensure you don't block the microphone while making a call.
19.	USB port and charging port (multipurpose port)
20.	Headset jack

Swiping the Screen Properly

From time to time, you would need to interact with the screen of your phone by swiping it with your finger. If you don't swipe it properly, you may not get the expected result. You can swipe to perform the following actions:

1. Access the notification menu/quick settings

To access the notification menu/quick settings, swipe from the top of the screen. Please make sure you are starting from the top of the screen (around the earpiece/receiver area) to get the expected result. See the picture below.

2. Accessing the app screen

To access the applications screen, swipe up from the lower part of the screen. See the direction of the arrow below.

Tip: To go back to the home screen while on the applications screen, just swipe up or down from the middle (or around the middle) of the screen.

Get to Know Settings Tab

I am talking about settings tab under this section because I will be referring to this tab a lot.

The settings tab has many subsections and because of this, I will advise that you use the **Search** menu (denoted by the lens icon 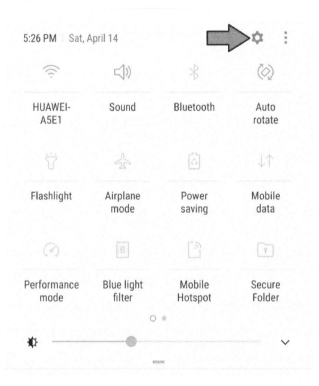) to quickly find what you are looking for. To use the setting's search feature, swipe down from the top of the screen and tap the settings icon (see the picture below).

Then tap on the search icon and type a keyword corresponding to the settings you are looking for. For example, if you are looking for settings relating to battery, just type **Battery** into the search bar. The result filters as you type.

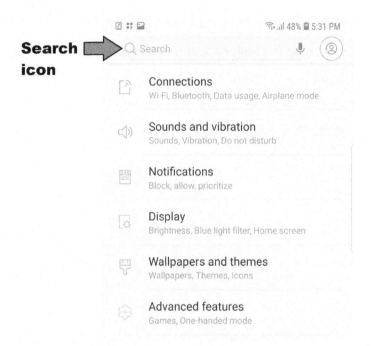

Tip: Samsung has added a feature that allows you to search the settings with your voice instead of typing. This appears cool and smart. To use this feature, just tap the microphone button and then say a word or a phrase. For example, you may say **battery** if you want to search for settings relating to battery.

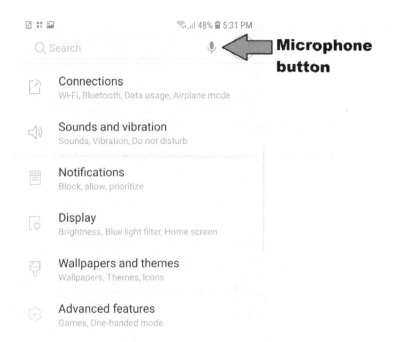

Connections
Wi-Fi, Bluetooth, Data usage, Airplane mode

Sounds and vibration
Sounds, Vibration, Do not disturb

Notifications
Block, allow, prioritize

Display
Brightness, Blue light filter, Home screen

Wallpapers and themes
Wallpapers, Themes, Icons

Advanced features
Games, One-handed mode

Microphone button

To speak another phrase or word, simply tap the **X** icon next to the present word/phrase, tap the microphone button again and speak a new phrase/word.

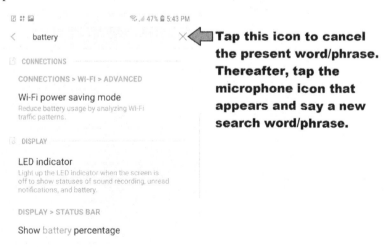

battery

CONNECTIONS

CONNECTIONS > WI-FI > ADVANCED

Wi-Fi power saving mode
Reduce battery usage by analyzing Wi-Fi traffic patterns.

DISPLAY

LED indicator
Light up the LED indicator when the screen is off to show statuses of sound recording, unread notifications, and battery.

DISPLAY > STATUS BAR

Show battery percentage

Tap this icon to cancel the present word/phrase. Thereafter, tap the microphone icon that appears and say a new search word/phrase.

Charging Your Device

If you are using your Samsung Galaxy S9/S9 Plus more often (especially if you use Wi-Fi more frequently), you may realize that you need to charge your phone every day. One of the coolest times to charge your device is when you are taking a shower, as you are not likely to be using it at the time.

Do you need to charge your phone before the first use?

Please see the answer on page 6.

To learn more on how to use your phone for a longer time on battery, please go to page 341.

To charge your Samsung Galaxy S9/S9 Plus:

1. When you first open your product box, you will notice that the power cord consists of two parts (i.e. the USB cable and the USB power adapter), connect these two parts together. See the picture below.

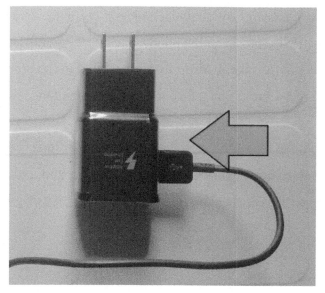

2. Connect the end of the USB cable to the charging port of your device, making sure that both the charging cable and the charging port on your device make a good and firm contact.

3. Plug the power adapter to an electrical outlet. When your phone is charging, a charging icon  will appear at the top of the screen. When your phone is fully charged, the battery icon will appear solid/full.

Note: After charging, you may need to apply a small force to remove the USB cord from the phone. Please be careful so that the phone does not mistakenly drop from your hand in the process.

4. To know the estimated charging time remaining, swipe down from the top of the screen and then tap **Settings** ⚙ > **Device Maintenance** > **Battery**. The charging time may be longer if you are using your device while charging it.

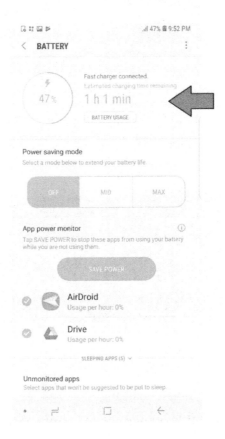

Tips:

- To extend the power of your device substantially, swipe down from the top of the screen and then tap **Settings** 🔧 > **Device Maintenance** > **Battery**. Under **Power saving mode** tab, tap MID or MAX and then tap **APPLY**.

 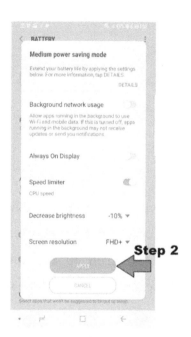

- There are some apps out there that will consume your battery even without using them. Interestingly, you can prevent these apps from this behavior. To do this, swipe down from the top of the screen and then tap **Settings** 🔧 > **Device Maintenance** > **Battery**. Under **App power monitor** tab, select the apps you want to prevent, and tap **SAVE POWER.**

In addition, if there is an app that you want to give unrestricted battery access to, tap **Unmonitored apps** (located at the bottom of the screen) and then tap **Add apps**. Select the app you want, and tap **DONE** located at the top of the screen.

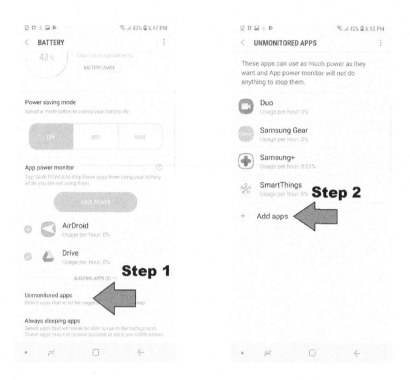

Tip: To remove an app from **Unmonitored apps** tab, swipe down from the top of the screen and then tap **Settings** ⚙ > **Device Maintenance** > **Battery** > **Unmonitored apps.** Then tap and hold the app(s) you want to delete. Tap **Delete** (located at the top of the screen) to remove the app from Unmonitored apps tab. Note that the app is not removed from your device, it is only removed from those apps that have unrestricted access to your battery.

In addition, if you do not want an app to consume your battery by running in the background, you can put it to sleep. To do this, swipe down from the top of the screen and then tap **Settings** ⚙ **> Device Maintenance > Battery > Always sleeping apps.** Then tap **Add apps**. Select the app you want, and tap **DONE** located at the top of the screen.

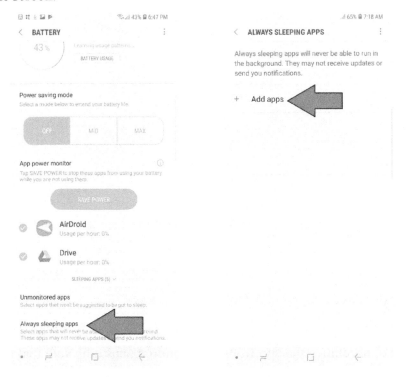

To remove an app from **Always sleeping apps** tab, tap **Always sleeping apps.** Then tap and hold the app(s) you want to delete. Tap **Delete** (located at the top of the screen). Note that the app is not removed from your device, it is only removed from those apps that are not able to run in the background.

Please note that not all app can be put to sleep using this method.

Warning: Please note that it is not advisable to use the multipurpose port while it is wet. If your phone has contact with water or any watery substance, please make sure you dry the multipurpose port before using it. Although Samsung Galaxy S9/S9 Plus is water resistant, it is not advisable at all to charge it while the device is wet. This may cause an electric shock or damage your device.

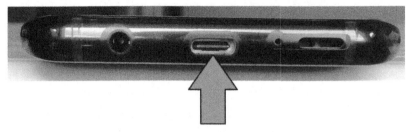

Multipurpose jack

Using the Fast Charging Feature

Your device is built with a battery charging technology that charges the battery faster by increasing the charging power. This feature can allow you to charge the device up to 50% in about 40-50 minutes. Interestingly, both Samsung Galaxy S9 and S9 Plus support fast wired charging and fast wireless charging.

Please note that using your phone while charging may affect the time your phone is going to take to make a complete charging cycle.

Tip: You can enable or disable the fast charging settings by going to Settings ⚙ > **Device Maintenance** > **Battery**. Then tap on menu icon ⋮ located at the top of the screen. Select **Advanced Settings** > **Fast cable charging**.

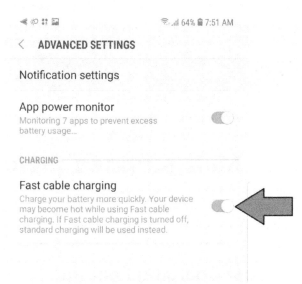

Furthermore, you might not be able to use the fast charging feature when you charge the battery using a standard battery/phone charger. To use **Fast Charging** on your device, you will need to connect it to a battery charger that supports Adaptive fast charging like the one that came with your device. To know if a battery charger supports this feature, check the charger for *Adaptive fast charging* inscription.

Although the fast charging technology on Samsung Galaxy S9/S9 Plus is a cool feature, it may still be affected by factors like the temperature of the phone. If the device heats up for one reason or the other, the charging speed may decrease.

What About the Wireless Charging?

Samsung Galaxy S9/S9 Plus has a built-in wireless charging feature and this means that you can charge your device's battery using a wireless charger (sold separately).

To charge your device wirelessly:

- Connect the power adapter that came with your wireless charger (sold separately) to the charging port on your wireless charger. Thereafter, plug it to a wall socket.
- If you are using your wireless charger for the first time, remove any protective nylon from the surface of the wireless charger. Then, place your mobile device on the wireless charger following the instructions provided by the manufacturer of the wireless charger. Please note that if you connect a charger to your mobile device during wireless charging, the wireless charging feature may be unavailable.

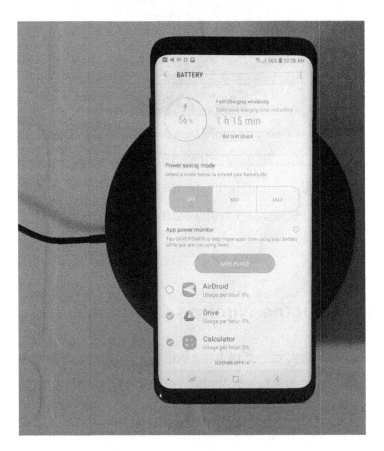

In addition, depending on the type of the wireless charger you are using, charging wirelessly may take a longer time when compared to using a cable. This means that if you want to charge your device faster, consider using a cable.

Inserting and Managing SD Card/SIM Card

Samsung Galaxy S9/S9 Plus supports the use of external memory card.

To insert memory card or SIM Card:

1. Locate the SIM and SD Card tray on the top edge of the device and gently insert the eject tool included with your phone into the eject hole (located at the top edge of your phone). Then push until the tray pops out. *Please note that you may need to apply small force before the tray pops out.*

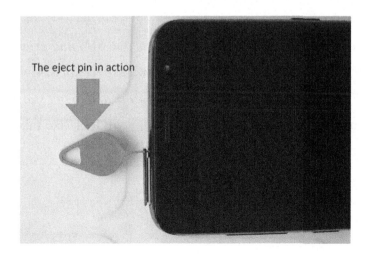

The eject pin in action

2. Pull out the tray gently from the tray slot and place the SIM Card on its tray and the SD Card on its tray. Make sure the metallic contacts on the SIM and the SD Card are facing down.

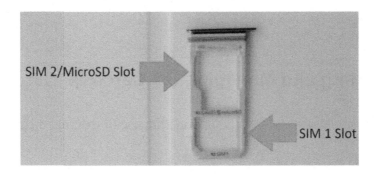

Hints: *Please note that SIM 2 may not be available on your phone if you don't buy the dual SIM version. In addition, if you are using the dual SIM version, you may not be able to use a second SIM and the external memory card at the same time. This is because both the second SIM (SIM 2) and the external memory card use the same space.*

*However, you may still be able to get a second SIM and external memory card to work simultaneously if you use a dual SIM adapter. Just search for **dual SIM adapter** on amazon.com to get started.*

After inserting the SIM(s), the whole setup will look like this. See the picture below.

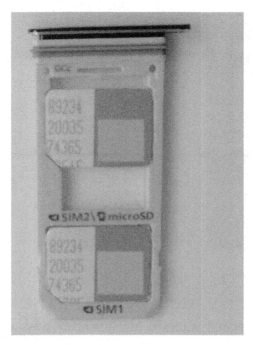

3. Slide the card tray back into the slot.

4. Please note that if the SIM Card or the memory card is not inserted properly, your phone might not recognize it. Please endeavor to follow the instructions above to avoid this.

5. To locate the memory card after inserting it, swipe up from the bottom of the screen, and tap **Samsung** folder > **My Files**, and then tap the **SD Card** folder.

Note: Since Samsung Galaxy S9/S9 Plus device is water resistant, you may be tempted to drop it in water at one time or the other. Please make sure that you fully insert the card tray into the tray slot before dropping the phone inside water so as to prevent liquid from entering your device.

As a rule, you must always make sure you prevent water from entering the inner compartment of the phone. Therefore, please make sure you properly close any slot you have opened on your phone before inserting it into water.

Hint: When the memory card is properly installed, you should see the memory card icon on the status bar at the top of the screen.

To remove the SD Card:

1. Swipe down from the top of the screen and select the settings icon  .

2. Tap **Device Maintenance**

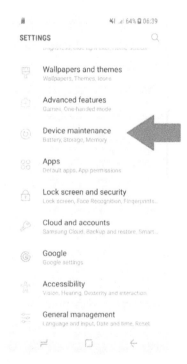

3. Tap **Storage.**

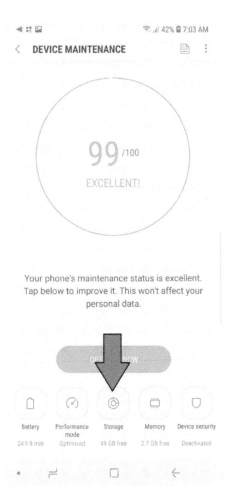

4. Tap the **menu icon** (the three dots icon located at the top of the screen).

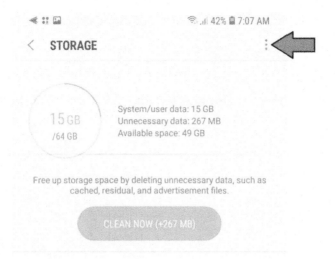

5. Tap **Storage settings**

6. Tap **Unmount icon** and gently open the SD Card slot using the ejection pin (as you have done above). Close the SD Card slot when you are done removing the memory card.

Please note that if you unmount the memory card without removing it from your device, you will need to mount it before it can be accessed again. To mount your memory card, follow the steps one to five above and then tap **Unmounted** and then select **Mount** when prompted.

Encrypt SD Card

You may wish to encrypt your memory card for extra security.

- From the Home screen, swipe up from the bottom of the screen and tap **Settings.**
- Tap **Lock screen and security**
- Scroll down and tap **Encrypt SD card**.

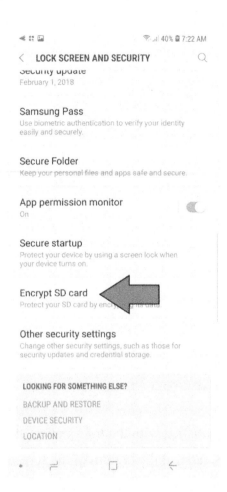

Security update
February 1, 2018

Samsung Pass
Use biometric authentication to verify your identity
easily and securely.

Secure Folder
Keep your personal files and apps safe and secure.

App permission monitor
On

Secure startup
Protect your device by using a screen lock when
your device turns on.

Encrypt SD card
Protect your SD card by enc...

Other security settings
Change other security settings, such as those for
security updates and credential storage.

LOOKING FOR SOMETHING ELSE?

BACKUP AND RESTORE

DEVICE SECURITY

LOCATION

- Please read all the onscreen information that appears.

<   **ENCRYPT SD CARD**

You can encrypt SD cards. Encrypted SD cards can only be read on the device used to encrypt them. Tap ENCRYPT SD CARD to start the encryption process.

Encryption could take an hour or more. Before you start, make sure that the battery is charged and keep the device plugged in until encryption is complete. During the encryption process, the SD card cannot be used. If your device is reset to factory default settings, it will be unable to read encrypted SD cards.

Read all the information above

- If you are satisfied with the information, then tap **Encrypt SD card** located at the bottom of the screen and follow the onscreen instructions to encrypt all data on your memory card.

When you encrypt your memory card, you may need a numeric PIN or password to decrypt your SD card when you first access it after switching on your device. In addition, *please note that encrypting a memory card may make it unreadable on another device.*

Formatting the memory card

1. Swipe down from the top of the screen and select the settings

   icon .

2. Tap **Device Maintenance**

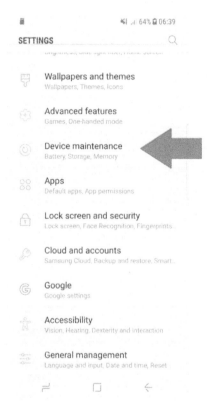

3. Tap **Storage.**

4. Tap the **menu icon** (the three dots icon located at the top of the screen).

5. Then select **Storage settings**

6. Tap **SD card**. (Please make sure you are tapping SD card and not the unmount icon next to it).

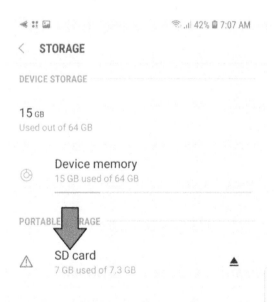

7. Tap **Format**, read the onscreen information and then tap **Format**.

Please note that formatting a memory card will cause you to lose all the files stored on the memory card and you may need to backup your files before initiating this process.

To transfer apps from internal storage to SD Card:

1. Swipe down from the top of the screen and tap **Settings** .

2. Tap **Apps**.

3. Tap the app you want to transfer.

4. Select **Storage** from the options that appear.

5. Next to the name of the app you want to transfer, tap **Change**.

Please note that this option may not be available for all apps. In fact, I have noticed that the "change" option is not available for most of apps that came with the phone.

6. Tap **SD card.**

7. Tap **Move** located at bottom of the screen and wait for the process to complete.

Tip: You may consider removing temporary files from your device to free up space. From the Home screen, swipe up from the bottom of the screen and tap **Settings** ⚙️ > **Device Maintenance**. Tap **Storage** and tap **Clean Now**.

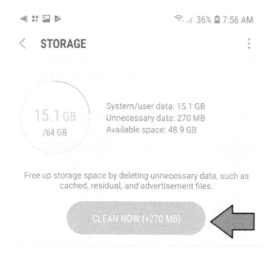

Please note that using this method may clear cached data for all apps.

Tip: If your phone is hanging or misbehaving, consider cleaning the memory. To do this, from the Home screen, swipe up from the bottom of the screen and tap **Settings** 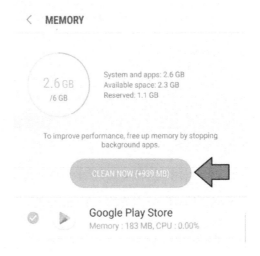 > **Device Maintenance**. Tap **Memory** and tap **Clean Now.**

Maintaining the Water and Dust Resistance

Although your Samsung Galaxy S9 and S9 Plus are water and dust resistant, there are few things you still have to put at the back of your mind so that you don't spoil your phone. Some of the things you have to know are discussed below:

- Even though your device is water resistant, you can't still immerse the device in water deeper than 1.5 m and/or keep it submerged for more than 30 minutes.

- The screen of your device may not respond properly while under water or wet. I will advice that you clean it with a dry towel to get the full functionality.

- It is not advisable to put your device under water moving with force such as tap water. This is because water may get into the inner part of your device in the process.

- While the phone's screen is wet, you may not enjoy the optimal function of your device as you should. You may need to clean it with a dry towel to make it work properly.

- To avoid electric shock, please don't charge your device while it is wet or while it is under water.

- Avoid putting your phone in a liquid other than water. In addition, avoid putting your phone inside salt water or ionized water.

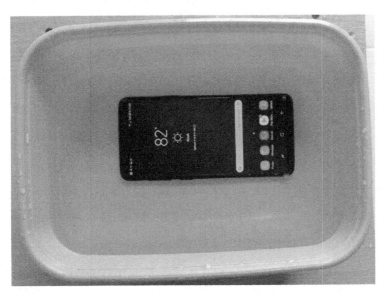

Note: Samsung Galaxy S9/S9 Plus may not respond to touch while under water but it should respond to touch immediately you take it out of water. But don't forget that you can't drop it inside water while the SIM/memory slot is opened. In addition, please don't charge your phone while it is wet to avoid electric shock.

Moving Your Items from Your Old Phone to Your Galaxy S9/S9 Plus

You can move your files to your new phone by following step(s) mentioned below:

- The easiest way to transfer your items from your old phone (Android Phone or IOS Phone) to your new Samsung Galaxy S9/S9 Plus is through the use of USB connector (On-the-Go

(OTG) connector) and a USB cable. To use this method, please follow the instructions below:

Please make sure you download and install Smart Switch app on your old phone before you begin the transfer process. Smart Switch can be downloaded from Google Play Store. In addition, this method of data transfer consumes large amount of energy, make sure your phone is fully charged before initiating this process.

To transfer content via cable:

- Plug the USB connector (On-the-Go (OTG) connector) that came with your device into the multipurpose jack of your device.

 **OTG Connector**

- Then connect your device and the old phone using a USB cable. Please note that you are to select Media device (MTP) option on your old phone if prompted. The whole connection will look like this (see below). *Please note that you may need to download, install and open Samsung Smart Switch Mobile on your old phone to complete this process.* **Samsung Smart Switch Mobile** app can be downloaded from Google Play Store.

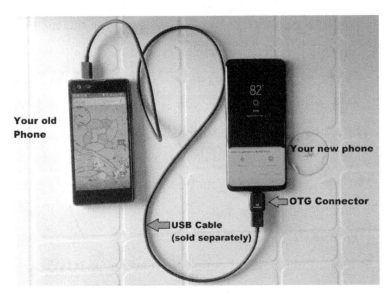

Your old Phone

Your new phone

OTG Connector

USB Cable
(sold separately)

- When prompted, tap **Smart Switch** and then select **Just Once**. If you are not prompted, disconnect the cable, then reconnect.

- Tap **Start**.

- Tap **Agree** if you agree with the terms/condition.

- Read the onscreen information and tap **OK** if you agree with the information.

- On the old phone open **Samsung Smart Switch Mobile** app and follow the prompts.

- Tap **Receive** on your Samsung S9/S9 Plus.

- Your device will recognize the old phone and a list of data you can transfer will appear. Select what you want to transfer and tap **Transfer.**

- Follow the on-screen instructions to complete the data transfer process.

- Alternatively, if the USB connector and the USB cable are not accessible, you can send items from your old phone to your new phone wirelessly using Smart Switch app. Please note that you will need to download and install **Samsung Smart Switch Mobile** app on your old phone to complete this process. **Samsung Smart Switch Mobile** app can be downloaded from Google Play Store.

  To transfer content wirelessly:

  - On your device, swipe down from the top of the screen and tap Settings icon ⚙ , tap **Clouds and Accounts** and then tap **Smart Switch**. Thereafter, tap **Start > Agree > OK > Wireless > Receive > Android**.

  - Open the **Smart Switch** app on your old phone.

  - Tap **Start** and tap **Agree**.

  - Tap **Wireless.** Then the Smart Switch app should then try to establish connection. If prompted, tap **Accept.**

    Please note that you may need to download and install Smart Switch app on your old phone if you don't have it. If you are using Android, **Samsung Smart Switch Mobile** can be downloaded from Play Store.

  - On your old phone, select those items you want to transfer, and tap **Send**.

- Follow the on-screen instructions on both your S9/S9 Plus and the old phone to complete the transfer process.

- When the transfer process is complete, tap **Close App**.

- I would like to mention that you can also transfer items from your old phone to your new device using memory card. All you have to do is to insert a memory card into your old phone, transfer your content to the memory card, remove the memory card and then place it inside your Samsung Galaxy S9/S9 Plus.

- Lastly, you can transfer your items from your old phone to your new phone by using cloud storage. For example, you can use OneDrive App. To do this, add files to OneDrive app on your old phone so that you can access them from your Samsung Galaxy S9/S9 Plus. To move a file to OneDrive, just drag and drop or send the files to your OneDrive folder. The files will be uploaded to OneDrive when you have an internet connection on that device.

Once the files are on your OneDrive, you can access them on your Samsung Galaxy S9/S9 Plus by opening OneDrive app. To avoid any problem while trying to access your files, please ensure that you are connected to a browsing network while trying to access OneDrive.

Please note that you may need to download OneDrive app to your phones to use this method.

Using the Touch Screen

Your phone's touch screen allows you to easily select items and perform functions. With the touch screen, you may operate your phone like a pro.

Notes:

- Do not press the touch screen with your fingertips, or use sharp tools on the touch screen. Doing so may cause malfunctioning.

- Do not allow the touch screen to come into contact with other electrical appliances. This may cause the touch screen to malfunction.

- When the touch screen is wet, endeavor to clean it with a dry towel before using it. The touchscreen may not function properly when wet.

- For optimal use of the screen, you may need to remove screen protector before using it. However, a good screen protector should be usable with your phone.

You may control your touch screen with the following actions:

Tap: Touch once with your finger to select or launch a menu, application or option.

Tap and hold: Tap an item and hold it for more than a second to open a list of options.

Tap and drag: Tap and drag with your finger, to move an item to a different location in the application grid/list.

Pinch: Place two fingers far apart, and then draw them closer together.

Hint: If you are using screen protector, you may consider increasing the touch sensitivity of your phone for optimum usage. To do this, swipe up from the bottom of the screen and tap **Settings** > **Advanced Features > Touch sensitivity.** Then tap the indicator switch next to **Touch sensitivity**.

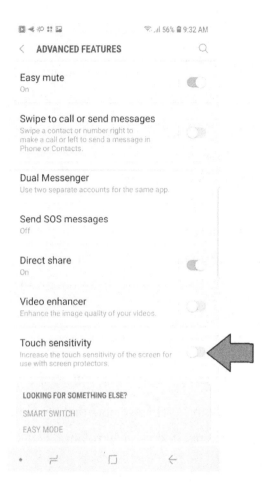

Easy mute
On

Swipe to call or send messages
Swipe a contact or number right to
make a call or left to send a message in
Phone or Contacts.

Dual Messenger
Use two separate accounts for the same app.

Send SOS messages
Off

Direct share
On

Video enhancer
Enhance the image quality of your videos.

Touch sensitivity
Increase the touch sensitivity of the screen for
use with screen protectors.

LOOKING FOR SOMETHING ELSE?

SMART SWITCH

EASY MODE

➢ **To Lock or Unlock the touch screen**

When you do not use the device for a specified period, your device turns off the touch screen and automatically locks the touch screen so as to prevent any unwanted device operations and also save battery. To manually lock the touch screen, press the power key.

To unlock, turn on the screen by pressing the power key (or double

tap the home button ▢) and then swipe in any direction. If you

have already set a lock screen password, you will be prompted to

enter the password instead of swiping.

Note: You can change the lock screen method on your phone,

please refer to page 134 to learn how to do this.

Rotating the touch screen

You phone has a built-in motion sensor that detects its orientation. If

you rotate the device, the screen should automatically rotate

according to the orientation.

> ➤ **To activate or deactivate screen rotation**

To quickly disable or enable screen rotation, swipe down from the

top of the screen and tap ⟲. Please note that when the screen

rotation icon appears grey, then screen rotation is disabled.

Using the Dedicated Back Button

You may use the dedicated back button (see the picture below) to view the previous page or go back to a previous menu. Back button can also be used to close a dialog box, menu, or keyboard.

In addition, you may use the dedicated back button on your device to get out of any page when you are done with the page and you don't see the done option.

Hint: Back button is one of the components of navigation bar. To learn how to manage navigation bar like a pro, please go to page 97.

Using the In-APP Back Button

There are some apps that give you the opportunity to go back to the

previous screen using the in-app back button ⟨ . When available, this button can be found at the upper left part of the screen.

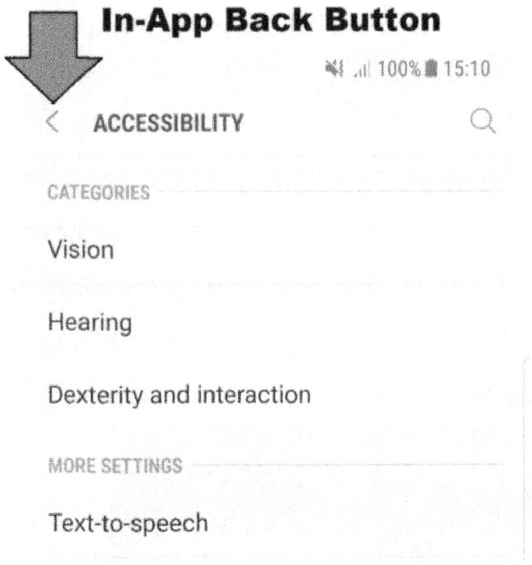

In-App Back Button

ACCESSIBILITY

CATEGORIES

Vision

Hearing

Dexterity and interaction

MORE SETTINGS

Text-to-speech

Getting to know the Menu icon

The menu icon is the three dots icon ⋮ that usually appears at the top of the screen when you open an app. This icon can also be called **hidden options icon**. This is because it contains more options about an app or item.

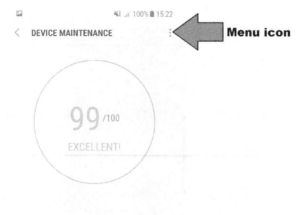

Your phone's maintenance status is excellent.
Tap below to improve it.

Hint: Whenever you are thinking of accessing more options when using an app/item or you are thinking of using an app in a new way, just tap on the menu icon.

Getting to know the Home Screen

From your home screen, you can view your phone's status and access applications. Scroll left or right to see different apps on the home screen. Please note that the home screen usually has many screens and you can add more screens to the home screen by tapping on +. More on this shortly.

Home Screen Layout:

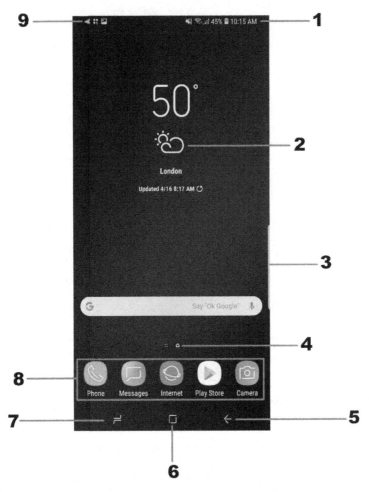

Number	Function
1.	**Status icons**: These icons tell you more about your device. For example, if the Wi-Fi is turned on, you would see the Wi-Fi status icon on this top right part of the screen.
2.	**Weather widget**: This widget may not be visible if you have not allowed it, to make weather

	widget visible, while on Home screen, tap and hold the screen and select **Widgets.** Swipe the screen until you see **Weather** and tap it. Then tap and hold **Weather** widget and move it to the desired home screen.
3.	**Edge Handle**: Swipe left on this handle to display edge icons.
4.	**Home Screen Indicator:** This indicates which home screen is currently visible
5.	**Back Button.**
6.	**Home Button**
7.	**Recent App button**
8.	**App shortcuts**: Tap any of these icons to launch the corresponding app.
9.	**Notification icon**: When you see a notification icon appearing at the top left part of the screen, simply swipe down from the top of the screen to learn more about this notification icon or see the notification detail.

Managing the Home Screen

To get more out of the home screen, you will need to perform some tweaks. To customize the home screen to your taste:

- While on the home screen, place your two fingers on the screen and then move them closer, or tap and hold an empty space on the home screen. To go to the home screen from

any screen, press the home button .

- Then you will see a screen that looks like the one below:

- You can perform any of the following actions:
  - **Add a screen**: To do this, swipe left until you see the plus/Add (**+**) icon. Tap this icon to add a new screen.

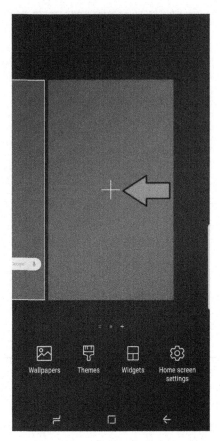

In addition, you can add app icons to a home screen. To do this, tap and hold an app icon on the applications screen and then select **Add to Home**.

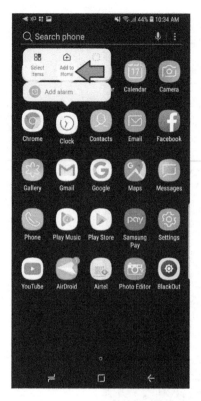

To move an app icon from one home screen to
another, tap, hold and drag the app icon to the edge of
the screen and wait for the screen to turn. Do this
until you get to the desired screen and then lift your
finger.

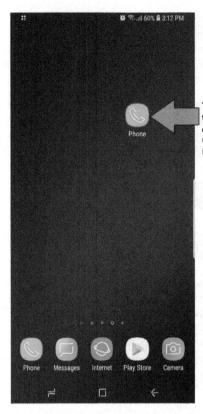

Tap and hold the app icon you want to move, then move it to the right edge or left edge of the screen until the page turns. When the app icon is in right position, lift your finger.

o **Remove a screen**: To do this, swipe left until you see the home screen you want to remove. Then tap the **Delete** icon located on top of the screen you want to delete.

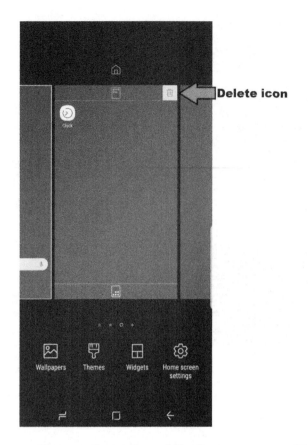

Delete icon

○ **Change the order of the home screens:** To do this, tap and hold a screen and drag it to the edge of the screen until the page turns. When the home screen is in the right position, lift your finger.

Tap and hold the screen you want to move, then move it to the right edge or left edge of the screen until the page turns. When the screen is in right position lift your finger.

To easily access a home screen, you may consider setting it as your **main** home screen. Please see below.

o **Set a screen as the main home screen:** To do this, swipe left or right until the screen is visible and then tap the **Home button** located at the top of the screen. When a screen is your main home screen, the home screen button appears bold.

Tip: To access the home screen at any point in time, press the dedicated home button [⬜].

- **Bixby Home**: To access Bixby home, swipe right. To enable or disable this feature, tap the status switch. To learn more about Bixby, please go to page 178.

Tip: To move out of a setting when you are done, tap the back button.

Back button

Hint: Do you want to increase or decrease the number of apps that appear in a row on the Home screen? If yes, go to page 77-79 to learn more.

Add/Remove an app shortcut to the home screen

You can add apps/items to the home screen so that you can easily access them anytime.

To do this:

1. Access the app screen by swiping up the screen while on the home screen.

2. While in the app screen, tap and hold an app icon, and then select **Add to Home**.

3. To move an app icon to a new location on the home screen, simply tap, hold and drag it to that location.

4. To remove an app icon from the home screen, tap and hold the app icon you want to remove and then select **Remove from Home**. Please note that removing an app icon from the home screen does not uninstall the app, it merely removes it from the home screen.

Managing the home screen widget

Widget is a small item that allows you to control an app in a special way. Widgets display information and invite the user to act in special ways.

To add a widget to a home screen:

1. While on the home screen, place your two fingers on the screen and then move them closer, or tap and hold an empty space on the home screen. To go to the home screen from any screen, press the home button  .

2. Tap on **Widgets** located at the bottom of the screen.

3. Swipe left or right to see the available widgets and select the one you like. Tap and hold a widget from the list of the widgets that appear, drag it to a home screen and release it.

4. To move a widget to a new location, tap, hold and drag the widget to the desired location. Tap outside the widget to save the changes.

5. To remove a widget from the home screen, tap and hold the widget and then select **Remove from Home screen**.

6. To resize a resizable widget, touch and hold, then release the widget. Then drag the rectangular blue outline to your desired size. Tap outside of the widget to save the changes. *Please note that you may not be able to resize all widgets.*

Rectangular outline

In addition, please note that you may not be able to adjust the size of some widgets vertically.

Managing the home screen theme

1. While on the home screen, place your two fingers on the screen and then move them closer, or tap and hold an empty space on the home screen. To go to the home screen from any screen, press the home button .

2. Tap **Theme** located at the lower side of the screen, and tap **Start.** If prompted, tap **Allow**, if you agree to the request.

3. Choose a theme. *Please note that you may need to agree to Terms and Conditions before you can access themes.*

4. To search for themes, tap the search button 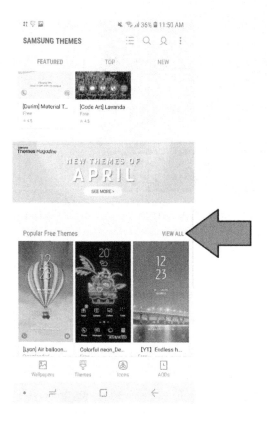 located at the top of the screen. Type a search phrase and hit the search icon on the virtual keyboard.

5. To see all your themes, tap **VIEW ALL.**

6. When you have seen the theme you like, tap the theme, and tap **Download**.

7. Wait for the theme to finish downloading and tap **Apply** (See below).

Step 6　　　　　　**Step 7**

8. To change the theme to the default one, open themes as described in step 1 and 2 above. Then tap the default theme and tap **Apply**.

Default theme

Please note that visual elements such as colors, icons, and wallpapers, may change depending on the selected theme.

Managing the home screen wallpaper

This option allows you to change the wallpaper settings for the Home screen and the locked screen.

1. While on the home screen, place your two fingers on the screen and then move them closer, or tap and hold an empty space on the home screen. To go to the home screen from any screen, press the home button ⬜.

2. Tap on **Wallpapers** located at the bottom of the screen.

3. To search for wallpapers, tap the search button 🔍 located at the top of the screen. Type a search phrase and hit the search icon 🔍 on the virtual keyboard.

4. To see all your wallpapers, scroll down and tap **VIEW ALL**.

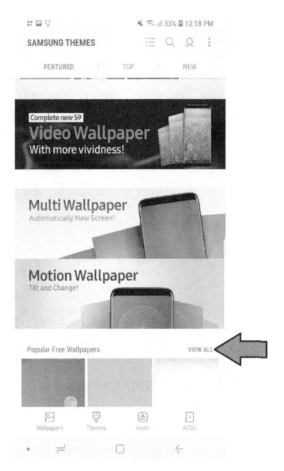

5. When you have seen the wallpaper you like, tap **Download** and then tap **Apply**.

6. Choose whether you want the wallpaper to appear on the **home screen, lock screen, or home and lock screens**.

7. Tick **Motion Effect**, if you want to give your wallpaper a motion effect.

Please note that "motion effect" may not be available if you choose "lock screen" in step 6 above.

8. Tap **Set as Wallpaper.**

Please note that you may be prompted while trying to apply a wallpaper, just read the information shown to you and agree if you like.

What about the screen grid?

The screen grid option allows you to choose the number of app icons that is displayed in a row on your home screen.

1. While on the home screen, place your two fingers on the screen and then move them closer, or tap and hold an empty space on the home screen. To go to the home screen from any screen, press the home button ▢.

2. Tap **Home screen settings**.

3. Tap **Home screen grid**.

4. Choose a dimension. 4x5 means there are four apps in a row and five apps in a column; 4x6 means there are four apps in a row and six apps in a column; 5x5 means there are five apps in a row and five apps in a column; and 5x6 means there are five apps in a row and six apps in a column.

5. When you are done picking a dimension, tap **Apply** (located
    at the top of the screen).

Tip: Alternatively, you can access the **home screen settings** by
performing the following actions:

- While on the home screen, swipe up the screen to access the applications screen.

- Tap the menu icon ⋮ and select **Home screen settings**.

To create a folder of items/apps on the Home Screen:

1. From the home screen or applications screen, tap and hold an app, then drag and drop it onto another item/app's icon to create a folder.

2. Tap **Enter folder name** and enter a name.

3. To change the color of the folder, tap the color icon ● and select a color.

4. To add another app, tap **ADD APPS** located at the bottom of the screen.

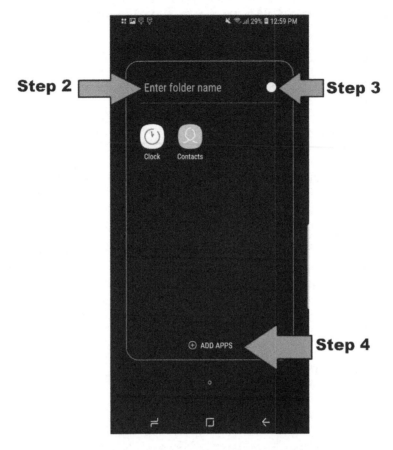

Step 2 → Enter folder name ← **Step 3**

Clock   Contacts

⊕ ADD APPS ← **Step 4**

5. When you are done customizing a folder, tap the **Done** button on the virtual keyboard or tap the back icon ← or both.

6. To remove an app from a folder, tap the folder, and then long-tap the app you want to remove and drag it out of the folder.
Please note that the folder is automatically deleted when it remains only one app in the folder.

Accessing and Managing Applications

To open an app:

1. From the home screen; swipe up from the bottom of the screen to access applications screen.

2. Tap the app of your choice

3. To go back to the app grid screen, press the back button

Accessing Recently Opened or Running Applications

1. Tap on the recent button ⇄ to show the recent apps window. This contains the list of all opened/running apps.

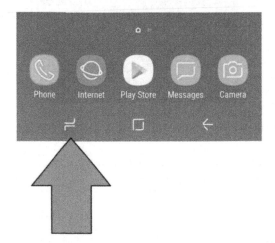

2. Tap an app to launch it, or tap the **X** icon to close it. To close all opened apps, tap **CLOSE ALL** located at the bottom of the screen.

Tip: You can lock an app so that it does not get closed when you tap

CLOSE ALL. To do this, tap the recent button ⌐ and select the

menu icon ⋮ located at the top of the screen. Then select Lock
apps.

Tap the padlock icon next to the app window you want to lock and select **DONE.** When the padlock icon is closed then the app window is locked.

*Please note that although a locked app window is not closed when you tap **CLOSE ALL**, you can still close it by swiping it to the right or left.*

Advice: Although Samsung Galaxy S9/S9 Plus can run many apps at a time, multitasking may cause memory problems, or additional power consumption. To avoid these, end all unused programs by closing the app.

Managing the applications screen

Selecting apps

You can select many apps to perform an action on all of them at the same time. To do this:

1. Tap and hold an app, and then tap **Select items.**

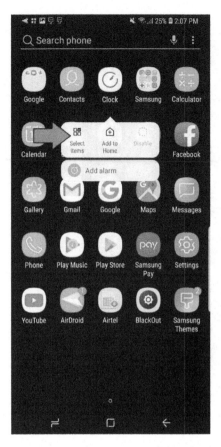

2. Then select all apps you want and choose an option at the top
   of the screen. If an option appears grey that means you can't
   use the option. For example, if your selection contains a
   folder, then the **Create folder** icon will appear grey because
   you can't put a folder inside another folder. Also, you can tap
   and hold an app in your selection to move them to another
   part of the screen. Or you can drag the selected apps up the
   screen to move them to the home screen and make them
   shortcuts.

Choose an option

Tip: Usually, when there is an app notification, a badge appears on the corresponding app icon. If an app has a badge, you can clear this badge by following the method below.

- Swipe down from the top of the screen to access the notifications screen.

- Dismiss the corresponding notification on the notification screen to clear the badge. For example, if AirDroid app has a badge, you will dismiss this badge when you dismiss its notification on the notification screen. You can dismiss a notification by swiping the notification towards right or left.

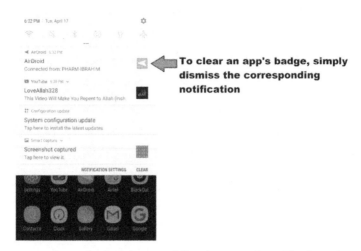

To clear an app's badge, simply dismiss the corresponding notification

Please note that a badge is a notification number displayed on an app icon, e.g.

Tip: To customize *app icon badges* settings, swipe down from the top of the screen and tap settings icon . Type in **app icon badges** into the search bar located at the top of the screen. The result filters as you type. Tap **app icon badges** from the results that appear.

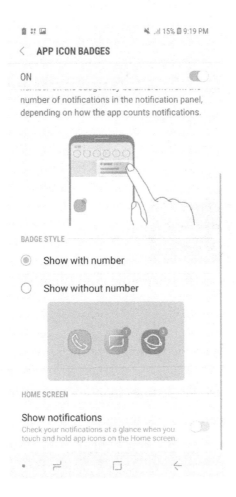

Showing the apps button

You can choose to show the apps button on the home screen.
To do this:

1. While on the home screen, swipe up the screen to access the applications screen.

2. Tap the menu icon ⁝ and select **Home screen settings**.

3. Tap **Apps button** and then choose **Show Apps button.** Then tap **APPLY** located at the top of the screen.

Arranging Application Alphabetically

1. While on the home screen, swipe up the screen to access the application screen.

2. Tap the menu icon ⋮ next to the search bar.

3. Tap **Sort** and choose an option.

Note: If you choose to arrange your apps/folders alphabetically, the folders will appear first.

Hiding applications

If you don't want your kid to access sensitive apps on your phone, you can hide them. For example, if you don't want your children to access your shopping app, you can hide it. However, please note that people may still be able to see your hidden apps, if they are tech savvy and they know the way.

To hide apps:

1. While on home screen, swipe up the screen to access the applications screen.

2. Tap the menu icon ⋮ and select **Home screen settings**.

3. Tap **Hide apps.** Then select the apps you want to hide, and tap **APPLY** located at the top of the screen.

4. To unhide the apps, just repeat the steps 1 to 3 above and unselect the apps you have selected before. Then tap **APPLY** located at the top of the screen.

Managing Applications

You can force-stop a misbehaving app. In addition, you can clear cache/data to clear errors in an app or to save phone memory.

To force-stop an app:

1. Swipe down from the top of the screen and tap settings icon

   ⚙ .

2. Swipe up and tap **Apps**.

3. Tap the app you want to manage.

4. To disable an app, tap **DISABLE.** Disabling an app may make such an app unavailable. To enable an app, repeat steps 1 to 3 above and tap **ENABLE**. *Please note that you may not be able to disable some apps on your phone. For example, you may not be able to disable some apps that came with your phone.*

5. To force-stop an app, tap **FORCE STOP.** Force-stopping an app is useful when an app is misbehaving or when it refuses to close. To access a force-stopped app again, just relaunch the app from the application screen.

6. To clear the cache or data of an app, tap **Storage** and then tap **CLEAR DATA** or **CLEAR CACHE.** *Please note that clearing data may cause you to lose settings, files and all*

other stored information on the app. Only clear the data of an app if you want to start using it as a new app.

Tip: If you don't see **Clear Data** in the step 6 above, then choose **Manage Storage.** When you choose **Manage Storage** option, you should be able to access Clear Data tab.

7. To manage the notification of an app, tap **Notifications** and choose an option.

8. To manage the permissions you have given to an app, scroll down and tap **Permissions** and choose an option.

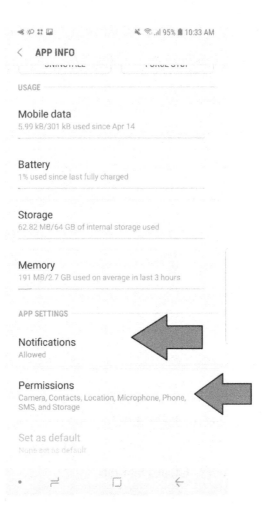

USAGE

Mobile data
5.99 kB/301 kB used since Apr 14

Battery
1% used since last fully charged

Storage
62.82 MB/64 GB of internal storage used

Memory
191 MB/2.7 GB used on average in last 3 hours

APP SETTINGS

Notifications
Allowed

Permissions
Camera, Contacts, Location, Microphone, Phone, SMS, and Storage

Set as default
None set as default

Hint: If an app is disturbing you with notifications and you want to quickly manage notification settings, just swipe down from the top of the screen and tap **NOTIFICATION SETTINGS.** Then use the status switch next to each app to manage their notifications. To learn more about phone notifications, see page 99.

Tip: Is there any confidential documents, files or items you want to make private so that only you can access them? If yes, do the following to protect them:

Swipe down from the top of the screen, and tap **Settings** ⚙ > **Lock screen and security** > **Secure folder**. Follow the onscreen instructions to complete the process.

Managing the Navigation Bar

The navigation bar is the bar at the bottom of your device screen. This bar comprises of back icon, home icon and recent apps icon. Interestingly, you can hide or unhide this bar. To manage notification bar:

1. Swipe down from the top of the screen and tap settings icon .

2. Then tap on the search icon.

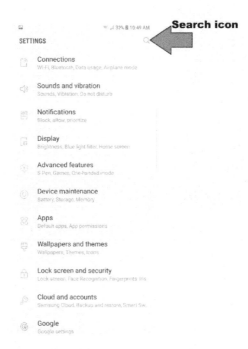

3. Type in **Navigation bar** into the search bar. The result filters as you type. Tap **Navigation bar** from the results that appear.

4. Choose an option from the Navigation bar settings screen.

5. To enable the **Show and hide button**, tap the status switch next to **Show and hide button.** When this is enabled you should be able to quickly hide or show the navigation bar by double tapping the small dot icon.

Status switch

Small dot icon

To show the navigation bar after hiding it, swipe in from the bottom of the screen.

Managing Phone Notifications

Notifications consume battery and it may be a source of disturbance occasionally. To manage notifications:

1. Swipe down from the top of the screen and tap settings icon

2. Then tap **Notifications**.

3. Use the status switch to manage notification for an individual app. To disable all notifications, tap the status switch next to **All apps** (located at the top of the screen.) To have an advanced management of notifications, tap **ADVANCED** and choose an app. You can use the advanced settings to manage apps that can give you notifications while **Do Not Disturb** (see page 294) is active.

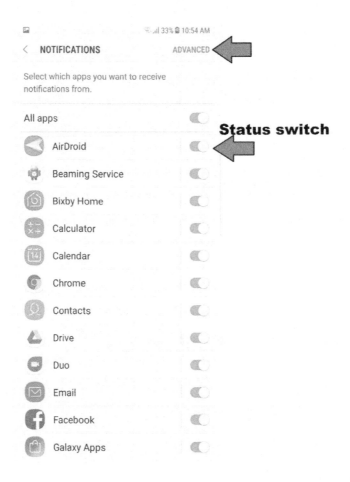

Tips: To manage notification sound on your phone, swipe down from the top of the screen, and tap **Settings** ⚙ > **Sounds and vibration** > **Notification sounds.** Then select **Silent** if you don't want a notification sound. To change your selection, choose a notification sound.

In addition, you can select whether you will see notification details or notification icon only on home screen. To do this, swipe down from the top of the screen and tap **Settings** ⚙ , type in **app icon badges** into the search bar located at the top of the screen. The result filters as you type. Tap **app icon badges** from the results that appear. Then scroll down and tap the status switch next to **Show notifications**, (see the picture below).

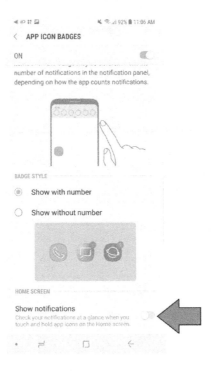

When you enable this option, you should be able to see your notifications at a glance when you touch and hold app icon on the Home screen.
If you don't want to see any form of notification icons/badges or details on your apps screen, tap the status switch next to **ON**.

Furthermore, you can quickly block a notification from the quick action menu. To do this, simply swipe down from the top of the screen, tap and hold a notification. Then tap the status switch to blocked notifications from the app in question. Thereafter, tap **Save** to register the changes. To view the detailed settings of a notification, select **DETAILS**.

Troubleshooting Tip: If you are not getting notification from an app (for example, if you are not getting notifications from Email app), these are the things to check:

1. Check whether you have not blocked notifications from this app. You can know this by following the steps on page 99/100.

2. Confirm that you have not disabled **Sync** function. To do this, swipe down from the top of the screen with two fingers. Then swipe left and see if **Sync** appears bold. If it appears bold, then it is enabled. Please note that if *Sync* is disabled you may not get some notifications.

3. If the first two steps above do not work, then make sure your phone is not restricting the app's battery usage. Restricting

the battery usage for an app may affect the ability of the app to get sync or use data. To know if an app has a restricted battery usage, go to **Settings** 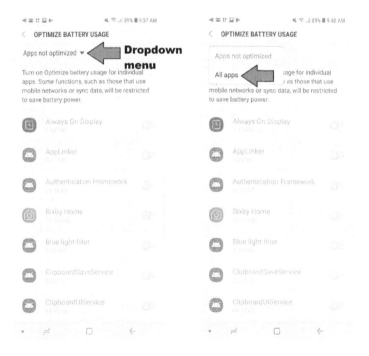 > **Apps** > **menu icon** (located at the top of the screen) > **Special access** > **Optimize battery usage**. Tap the dropdown menu and select **All apps**. Locate the app in question and make sure the indicator switch next to it is turned off.

Using the Multi Window/Split-Screen Function

Multi window is one of the coolest features of Samsung Galaxy S9/S9 Plus. Multi window allows you to put two apps side by side. *However, it is important to note that not all apps support multi window feature.*

Using Multi Window feature:

Before you start using multi-window/split-screen, I will advise that you enable *Use Recents button* feature. To do this:

1. Swipe down from the top of the screen and tap settings icon
   ⚙.

2. Tap **Advanced features.**

3. Scroll down and tap **Multi window**

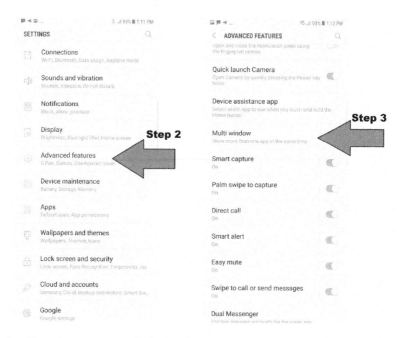

4. Tap the status switch next to **Use Recents button.**

MULTI WINDOW

Use Recents button
Touch and hold the Recents button to change the current app from full screen view to split screen view.

Use Recents button
Open and close apps in split screen view or use Snap window.

Pop-up view action
Off

Note that when this option is enabled, you will be able to change the current app from full screen view to split-screen view by pressing and holding Recent button ⌐⌐.

To use multi window feature:

1. Open an app that supports multi-screen (e.g. phone app).

2. Touch and hold the recent button ⌐⌐ and then tap **APPS LIST.**

3. Choose an app from the list that appears.

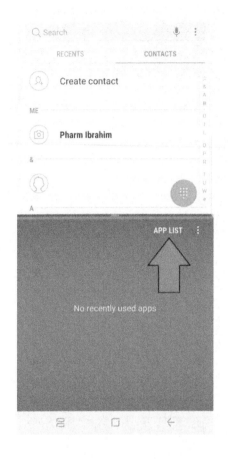

4. Alternatively, tap the recent button to open the list of recently used apps. Then tap the split-screen icon on the app you want to split. The app will launch in the upper window and the other recently used apps that support multi window will display below the launched app. Swipe up or down (if necessary) and select the second app.

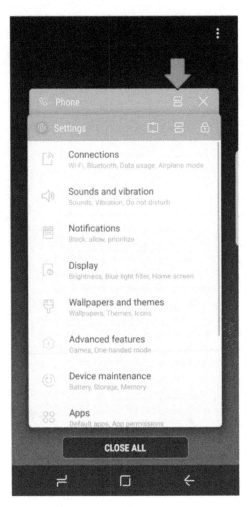

5. To adjust the size of an app window, tap the middle of the
    dividing line between the app windows (i.e. the straight line
    that appears between the two app windows) and drag it up or
    down. See the picture below.

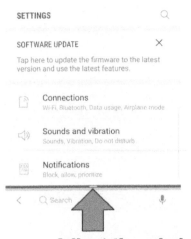

**Adjust the window by dragging
this small white icon**

No recent searches

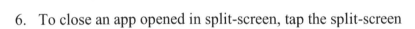

6. To close an app opened in split-screen, tap the split-screen

   icon ▤ and then tap the **X** icon next to the app you want to

   close. See below.

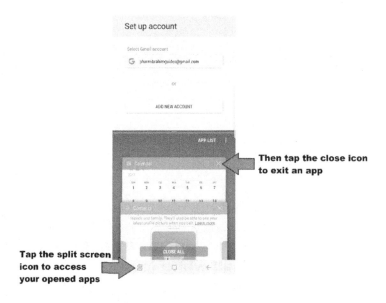

Then tap the close icon
to exit an app

Tap the split screen
icon to access
your opened apps

If you can't see the **X** icon, then the app may be locked. To unlock
the app, tap the padlock icon.

Padlock icon

7. To open another app in split-screen, tap the split-screen icon
, tap **APP LIST** and then select an app.

8. To exit multi window view, tap and hold the split-screen icon ⊟ (located at the bottom of the screen).

Using the Multi Window Controls

When using apps in the split screen view, tap the middle of the dividing line between the app windows to access multi window options.

To dismiss the multi window screen controls, tap the back button.

The Multi Window Options

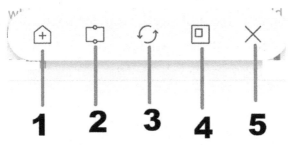

Icon	Function
1.	Tap this button to add the current app pair (i.e. the current two apps you are viewing) to the home screen. This will allow you to quickly access the two apps in the future.
2.	Tap this icon to move an app window to another part (usually the top part of the screen). When you tap this icon, a blue outline will appear. Adjust this blue outline as you wish to resize the window. When you are done resizing, tap **DONE** to effect the changes.
3.	Tap this icon to switch window positions i.e. move a lower app window to upper part of the screen and vice versa.
4.	Tap this to open an app in a pop-up windows or minimize an app.
5.	Tap this icon to close the currently active app and exit the multi windows screen.

Using the Minimize icon:

1. When using apps in the split-screen view, tap the middle of the dividing line between the app windows to access multi-window options.

Tap this

2. Tap the minimize icon ⬚ to minimize the currently active app; then tap and hold the upper part of the window next to the outline to drag the window from one part of the screen to another. To resize it however, tap, hold and move the outline as you wish.

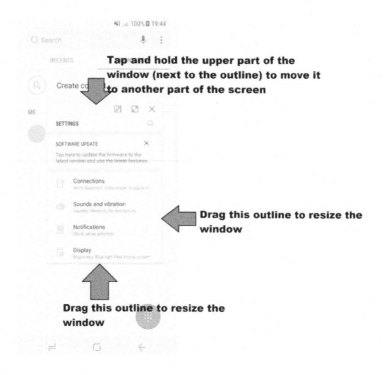

Tap and hold the upper part of the window (next to the outline) to move it to another part of the screen

Drag this outline to resize the window

Drag this outline to resize the window

3. Tap 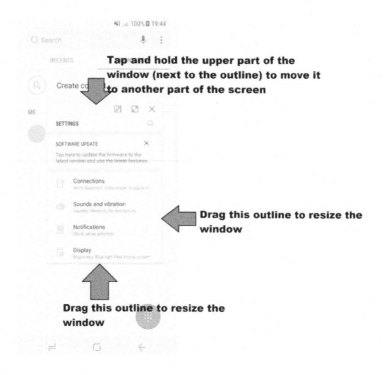 to minimize the app window to a small icon. This small icon can be dragged from one part of the screen to another when you tap, hold and move it.

4. To maximize the window to a full screen, tap the corresponding small icon and then tap . For example, if the app in question is settings app, tap the small icon representing the settings app and then tap the maximize button .

Understanding the Quick Settings menu

The Quick settings panel present on notification panel provides a quick access to device functions such as Wi-Fi, allowing you to quickly turn them on or off.

Tip: The app icon that is currently active in Quick settings menu will appear bold, so if you want to know whether you have enabled a feature or not, just check its boldness. For example, if you want to know if Bluetooth is on, swipe down from the top of the screen and see if the Bluetooth icon appears bold.

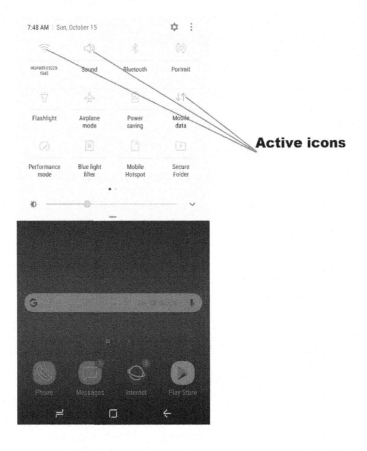

To view additional Quick settings:

1. Swipe down from the top of the screen to display the Notification panel.

2. Drag down the double dash == icon to see more icons (see the picture below).

Tip: To have a robust view of the Quick settings icons, swipe down from the top of the screen using two fingers.

To customize the Quick settings icons:

1. Swipe down from the top of the screen using two fingers.

2. Tap the menu icon ⋮ located at the top of the screen.

3. Tap **Button order.**

4. Tap, hold and drag any of the icons to change their positions.

5. To add an app to the Quick settings panel, drag the app from lower section of the screen (the gray area) to the top section of the screen.

6. To remove an icon from the Quick settings panel, drag the app icon to the lower section of the screen (the gray area).

6. Tap **DONE** located at the top of the screen to save the changes.

7. To restore the icons' arrangement to the default arrangement, tap **RESET** and then tap **DONE.**

Tip: To change the number of app icons that appear in a row/column in Quick settings menu, repeat steps 1 and 2 above. Then select **Button grid** and choose an option.

Customizing Your Phone

You can get more done with your phone by customizing it to match your preference.

To change your language:

1. Swipe down from the top of the screen and select settings

   icon ⚙ . Then scroll down and tap **General management.**

2. Tap **Language and input.**

3. Tap **Language**.

4. Tap **Add language**.

5. If you want to access a more robust list of languages, tap the

   menu icon ⋮ and then tap **All languages**.

6. Select a language from the list. If your chosen language is spoken in more than one country/region, select a country/region for your chosen language.

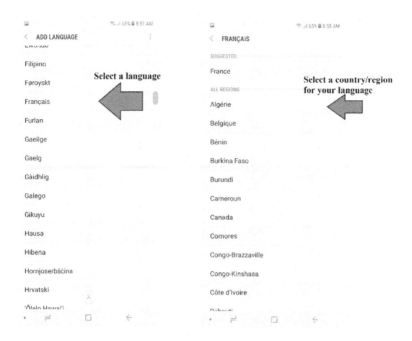

7. Using the v-like icon next to a language, tap and drag your preferred language to the number one position in the language list. Then tap **Apply** to set the language as the default language.

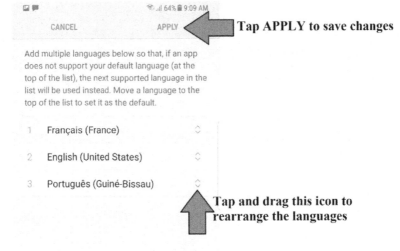

Tap APPLY to save changes

Add multiple languages below so that, if an app does not support your default language (at the top of the list), the next supported language in the list will be used instead. Move a language to the top of the list to set it as the default.

1 Français (France)

2 English (United States)

3 Português (Guiné-Bissau)

Tap and drag this icon to rearrange the languages

8. To delete a language, tap **DELETE** located at the top of the screen and tap the language you want to delete. Then select **DELETE** and tap **OK**. Please see below for details.

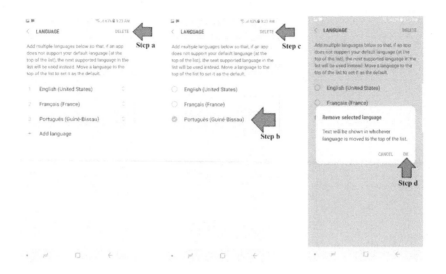

Selecting the Default Keyboard

1. Swipe down from the top of the screen and select settings icon ⚙. Then scroll down and tap **General management**.

2. Tap **Language and input.**

3. Tap **Default Keyboard** and then choose a keyboard. Please note that if you have not downloaded extra keyboards from Google Play Store, you may see only two options.

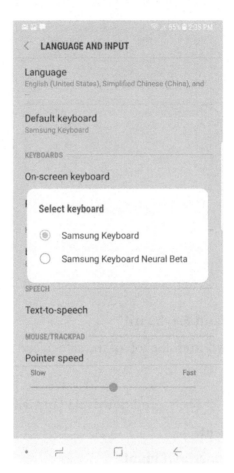

I would advise that you go to Google Play Store to download more keyboard(s). Just open Google Play Store app and search for **Keyboard.** Then choose a beneficial keyboard from the options that appear. After you have downloaded and installed a keyboard, then perform the following actions:

1. Swipe down from the top of the screen and select settings icon 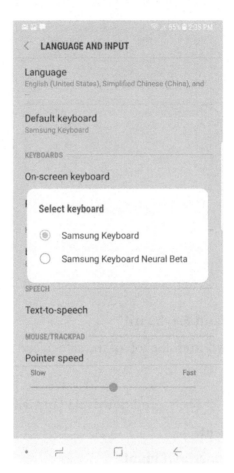 . Then scroll down and tap **General management.**
2. Tap **Language and input.**
3. Tap **On-screen keyboard**

4. Tap **Manage keyboards.**

5. Tap the status switch next to the keyboard you just installed to enable it. In this case, I have just downloaded and installed **SwiftKey Keyboard** from Google Play store. Please note that you can't disable Samsung Keyboard. It is enabled by default and it appears there is nothing you can do about this for now.

6. Tap the back button ← until you see **Language and Input** screen. Then tap **Default keyboard** and choose an option.

Hint: Your device comes preloaded with Samsung Keyboard, to customize this keyboard to your taste, swipe down from the top of the screen, and tap **Settings** ⚙ **> General management >** **Language and input > On-Screen Keyboard > Samsung keyboard.** Then tap any of the on-screen options. I would advise that you go through these options serially to have the best keyboard experience.

⟨   **SAMSUNG KEYBOARD**

Languages and types
English (US)

Smart typing
Predictive text, Text shortcuts, Keyboard
swipe controls

Keyboard layout and feedback
Keyboard toolbar, Keyboard size and layout, Custom
symbols, Key-tap feedback

Reset to default settings

About Samsung Keyboard

**Samsung Keyboard
Options**

⇄   ☐   ←

In addition, you can allow your keyboard to support more languages. To do this, swipe down from the top of the screen, and tap **Settings**

⚙ **> General management > Language and input > On-Screen Keyboard > Samsung keyboard > Languages and types > MANAGE INPUT LANGUAGES.** Then tap the status switch next to all the languages you want the keyboard to support.

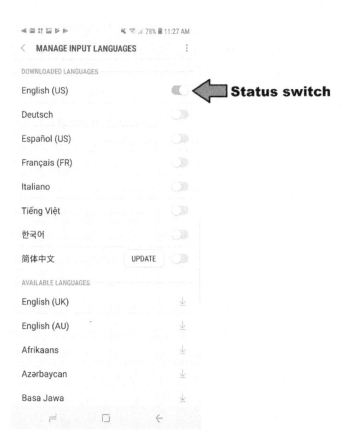

To change your keyboard language to any of the one selected above, swipe the space bar on the virtual keyboard to right or left until you see the language of your choice.

Swipe this to right or left

Set the Current Time and Date

Your device is built to update its time automatically, but you may need to manually set your time for one reason or the other. To manually set the time and date:

1. Swipe down from the top of the screen and select settings

   icon . Then scroll down and tap **General management.**

2. Tap **Date and time.**

3. To ensure that the time on your device is updated automatically, enable the status switch next to **Automatic date and time.** Please note that when this status switch is enabled, it would appear bold.

4. To set the time on your device manually or prevent your device from updating the time automatically, disable the status switch next to **Automatic date and time**, and then edit the time and date as you desire.

5. To manage the time zone settings, disable the status switch next to **Automatic date and time** and then tap **Select time zone.**

6. To use a 24 hours' time setting for your device, enable the status switch next to **Use 24-hour format**.

Note: When the status switch is on, it will appear bold.

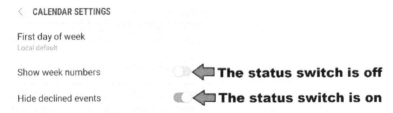

To Control Sounds and Vibrations

1. Swipe down from the top of the screen and select settings

   icon .

2. Tap **Sounds and vibration** and tap an option. For example, to mute the sound on your phone, tap **Sound mode** and then tap **Mute.**

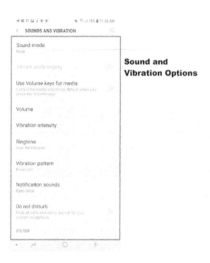

Sound and
Vibration Options

Adjusting the Volume of Your Phone

To adjust the volume of your phone, press the **Volume key**. The volume key is the long key located at the left side of your phone (when the phone is facing you).

Adjusting the Brightness of the Display

1. Swipe down from the top of the screen using your two fingers. Then drag the slider under the Quick action icons to adjust the brightness.

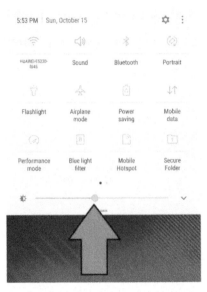

Hint: The brightness level of the display will affect how quickly the device consumes battery power. I would advise that you turn it reasonably low if you are very concerned about saving your battery. In addition, using your phone on high brightness for a long time may strain your eye.

To Set a Screen Lock Password or PIN

You can lock your phone by activating the screen lock feature.

Note: Once you set a screen lock, your phone will require an unlock code each time you turn it on or unlock the touch screen.

1. Swipe down from the top of the screen and tap settings

   icon ⚙ .

2. Tap **Lock screen and security** and then **Screen lock type**.

3. Tap a screen lock type you like.

4. If you choose **Password or PIN**, then enter the **password/PIN** you wish and follow the onscreen instructions

to complete the setup. In addition, you may choose **Pattern** or **Swipe.** If you don't want a lock screen, tap **None.**

Tip: You may also use your fingerprint or iris to unlock your phone. More on this in the next section (see page 142-151).

Entering a text

You can enter a text by selecting characters on the virtual keypad or by speaking words into the microphone using a voice command app.

To enter a text:

1. Enter a text by selecting the corresponding alphabets, symbols or numbers.
2. You can use any of the following keys:

Please note that the on-screen keyboard on your phone may be different from the one shown below. This is because the on-screen keyboard you see depends on the text input field you select. The one shown below is the one you should see when you want to compose a text message.

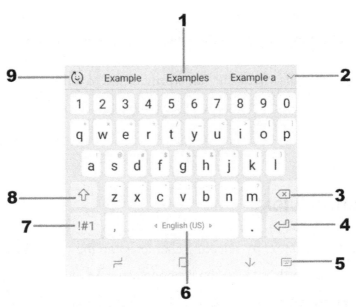

Number	Function
1.	**Predictive text bar** **Tip**: The phone has an auto replace feature, and as you type, your phone will give you text suggestions, the most likely suggestions will appear in blue on the predictive text bar. To use the suggestion that appears in blue, (the suggestion that appears at the center), tap the space bar. To use a different suggestion, tap on it. Please be informed that you can disable this auto replace feature, to do this, please see page 139.
2.	Tap on this to see more predictive texts or more settings.
3.	Clear your input/backspace
4.	Start a new line.

5.	Tap this icon to select a new keyboard type
6.	**Space bar**: you can swipe right or left to switch between input languages. To add input language, please go to page 129.
7.	Switch between Number/Symbol mode and ABC mode
8.	Change case
9.	**Option tab**: when you press and hold this button, you will gain an access to a list of icons/functions.

Hint: When you tap the option tab 😊 you will gain access to the following:

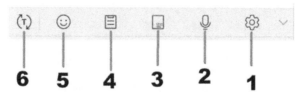

1. **Keyboard settings:** Tap this to access the keyboard settings.
2. **Voice input**: Enter text by voice.
3. **One-handed keyboard**: Tap this to be able to control the virtual keyboard using one hand. When you tap the **One-handed keyboard** button, you will see a keyboard that looks like the one below.

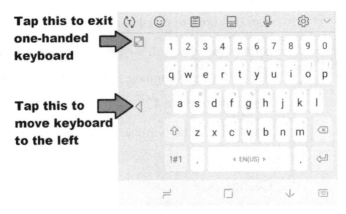

Tap this to exit one-handed keyboard

Tap this to move keyboard to the left

4. **Clipboard:** Tap this to add an item from the clipboard. After using an item on the clipboard, tap the arrow icon ↓ (located at the bottom of the screen) to exit.

5. **Emoticon**: Tap this to add emoticons to your texts.

6. **Option button:** Tap this to switch to predictive texts.

Tip: To learn how to manage the on-screen keyboard, please go to page 128. When you select two or more languages, you can switch between the input languages by swiping to the left or right on the space key.

Note: By default, you may notice that Samsung automatically replace your typed word with another one (a corrected one) when you press the space bar. While this option is cool, it may be

unwanted sometimes, to disable this function, go to **Settings** ⚙ > **General management > Language and input > On-Screen Keyboard > Samsung keyboard > Smart typing > Auto replace.** Then tap the status switch next to **English** (or your default language) to disable it.

To Copy and Paste a Text

While entering or reading a text, you can use the copy and paste options. To do this:

1. Tap and hold a word to display copy options. The icons below will show up after selecting a text or texts.

2. Drag ◖ or ◗ to select more texts.
3. Select **Copy** icon to copy or select **Cut** icon to cut the text onto the clipboard.
4. In another application or where you want to paste the text, tap and hold the text input field.
5. Select **Paste** icon to insert the text from the clipboard into the text input field. You can also tap the clipboard icon 🗒 to access the clipboard for more paste options.

Using the Voice Typing

1. Tap the option tab ☺ , and then select 🎤 .

2. Speak your text. Your device types as you speak.

3. To pause the voice typing, tap the screen.

4. To manage the voice typing option, swipe down from the top of the screen, and tap **Settings** ⚙ > **General management** and tap **Language and input**. Tap **On-Screen keyboard** and tap **Samsung voice input.**

5. To exit the voice typing, tap the arrow icon ↓ (located at the bottom of the screen).

Using The Special Features

Samsung Galaxy S9/S9 Plus came with special features that make it distinct. I will now explain how to use these features.

Using the Fingerprint Feature

One of the cool features on Samsung Galaxy S9/S9 Plus is Fingerprint. This allows you to unlock applications without entering boring passwords.

Registering your Fingerprint

Before you can start using your fingerprint on the device, you will need to first register your fingerprint. You have the chance of registering up to three fingerprints. In addition, you also have the option of registering a password as a backup.

To do this:

1. Swipe down from the top of the screen and select settings icon ⚙ .

2. Tap **Lock screen and security**.

3. Tap **Fingerprint scanner**.

4. Read the on-screen tips and tap **Continue**.

5. Tap an alternative lock method and follow the prompts. You will need this alternative lock method in some occasions. If you have set a lock screen before, then you just need to enter the lock PIN/Password/Pattern.

6. Place one of your fingers on the fingerprint reader located under the phone camera at the back of the phone, then lift it when the fingerprint is detected and read. You may need to repeat this several times.

Fingerprint scanner

7. To add another fingerprint, tap **Add** and follow the prompts.

8. When you are done adding your fingerprints, tap **Done.**

Renaming Fingerprints

1. Swipe down from the top of the screen and select settings icon .

2. Tap **Lock screen and security**.

3. Tap **Fingerprint scanner**.

4. Unlock the screen using the preset screen lock method and tap **NEXT**.

5. Tap the fingerprint you want to rename. For example, tap **Fingerprint 1.**

6. Enter a new name, and then tap **Rename**.

Tip: When renaming your fingerprint, make sure you use the name of the finger you registered. For example, you can use the name **Index finger** or **Forefinger**. This prevents unnecessary confusions.

Deleting Fingerprints

1. Swipe down from the top of the screen and select settings icon ⚙.
2. Tap **Lock screen and security**.
3. Tap **Fingerprint scanner**.
4. Unlock the screen using the preset screen lock method and tap **NEXT**.
5. Touch and hold the fingerprint you want to delete, and then tap **Remove**.

Setting a Screen Lock with Fingerprint

You can lock the screen with your fingerprint instead of using a pattern, PIN, or password.

1. Swipe down from the top of the screen and select settings

   icon .

2. Tap **Lock screen and security**.

3. Tap **Screen lock type**.

4. Unlock the screen using the preset screen lock method and tap **NEXT**.

5. Tap the status switch next to **Fingerprint**.

Using Fingerprints to Sign In to Accounts

Apart from using your fingerprint to unlock your device, you can also use it to access online features.

1. Swipe down from the top of the screen and select settings

   icon .

2. Tap **Lock screen and security**.

3. Tap **Fingerprint scanner**. Unlock the screen using the preset screen lock method and then do any of the following:

   a. Tap **Samsung Pass** to access your online accounts/apps using your fingerprint. To get started with this feature, just tap Samsung Pass and follow the prompts.

   b. Tap **Samsung Pay** to use your fingerprint for secured and fast payments with the Samsung Pay app. To get started with this feature, just tap Samsung Pay and follow the prompts. Samsung Pay may not be available in some locations in the world.

   c. Tap the switch next to **Fingerprint unlock** to enable or disable fingerprint security.

Troubleshooting the Fingerprint Scanner

If the fingerprint scanner is not responding, try any of the following:

1. Remove any phone case that may be covering the fingerprint reader located at the back of the phone.
2. Ensure that you are not using the tip of your fingerprint. Make sure to cover the entire Fingerprint reader with your finger.
3. If your finger has scars, try using another finger, this is because your device may not recognize fingerprints that are affected by wrinkles or scars.
4. Ensure the finger you registered with is used.

5. Make sure that your finger and the surface of the fingerprint scanner are clean and dry.

Iris Scanner

You can lock and unlock your phone using your iris.

1. Swipe down from the top of the screen and select settings icon ✿.

2. Tap **Lock screen and security**.

3. Tap **Iris scanner**. You may need to setup an alternative lock screen method or enter your lock screen information if you have already setup a lock screen.

4. Read the on-screen tips and tap **OK/Continue**.
   Please note that it is recommended that you keep the screen at least 8 inches away from your face to protect your eyes when using iris recognition.

5. Hold the phone 10 inches to 14 inches from your face. Make sure you are not wearing glasses. Follow the prompts to complete the registration.

6. After the registration, you will see some information telling you more about the Iris scanner. Read this information and tap next icon ⟩ located at the bottom of the screen. Finally, tap **OK** to go to Iris setting page.

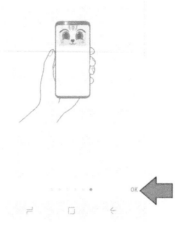

7. On the Iris setting page, tap an option to enable/disable it. To
   know what each option stands for, read the information under
   the option.

IRIS SCANNER

MANAGE IRISES

Remove iris data

Preview screen mask

IRIS VERIFICATION

Samsung Pass
Use your irises to verify your identity via internet and
other supported apps.

Samsung Pay
Use your irises to verify your identity when purchasing
content via Samsung services.

Iris unlock
Unlock your phone with your irises.

Iris unlock when screen turns on
Unlock your phone with your irises as soon as
the screen turns on, without swiping first.

Tips for using iris recognition

Tap an option

8. To remove Iris data, tap **Remove iris data** and tap **Remove**.

9. To get tips for using iris recognition, tap **Tips for using iris recognition**.

Troubleshooting the Iris Scanner

If the Iris scanner is not responding, try any of the following:

1. Remove any screen protector that may be covering the iris camera, LED sensor, or proximity sensor located above your screen (see page 7 and 8 for pictorial representation).

2. Ensure that you are not wearing glasses.

3. Ensure that you are not trying to use the Iris scanner under the direct sunlight.

4. Ensure that you hold the phone between 10 and 14 inches from your face.

5. Ensure you hold the phone to the level of your face/eyes.

Water Resistance

Another feature that makes Samsung Galaxy S9/S9 Plus unique is the water resistivity. You don't have to worry that your phone is going to get wet when you are drenched by the rain or inside a bathroom. To know more about water resistivity, please go to page 40.

Using the Always On Feature

The Always On feature allows you to display information, such as a clock, calendar, or image, on the screen when it is turned off. I personally love the fact that you can check the time with this feature even if the screen is off.

1. Swipe down from the top of the screen and select settings

   icon ⚙ .

2. Tap **Lock screen and security**.

3. Scroll down and tap **Always on display**.

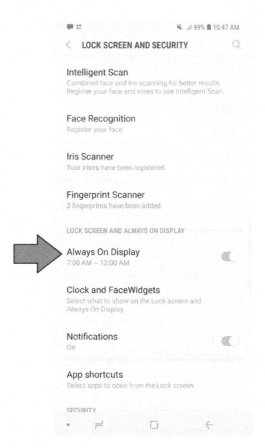

4. Tap On/Off switch to enable or disable Always on Display.

When you enable **Always on Display**, you can access the following:

a. **Content to show**: This feature allows you to choose the content to show when the screen is off. See the screenshot below.

b. **Show Always**: When this is enabled, the Always on Display is active every time. To customize when Always on Display will be active, tap the status switch next to **Show Always** and set a schedule.

Switch off "Show always" so that you can be able to set a schedule.

   c. **About Always on Display**: Tap this to view the current software version, update the app and check license information.

Good news: One interesting thing about Always On option is that it consumes a very low amount of battery energy.

Changing the Clock style/Calendar style/Image on "Always on Display"

You can choose the clock style, calendar style, image, or Edge clock to be displayed when Always on Display is active. To do this:

1. Swipe down from the top of the screen and select settings

   icon ⚙ .

2. Tap **Lock screen and security**.

3. Scroll down and tap **Clock and FaceWidgets**

4. Tap **Clock style**

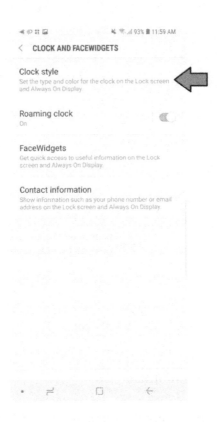

5. Scroll through the available clock style/calendar style/image thumbnails and choose one. If clock/calendar style thumbnails are not showing, tap **Type** (located at the bottom of the screen).

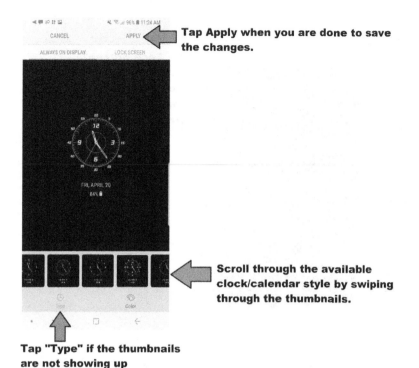

Tap Apply when you are done to save the changes.

Scroll through the available clock/calendar style by swiping through the thumbnails.

Tap "Type" if the thumbnails are not showing up

6. Tap **Color** ⬤ and select color of your choice.

7. Tap **Apply** located at the top of the screen to effect changes. Note that you may not be able to choose a clock, image or calendar to display if you choose **Home button** only under **Content to Show** on page 153.

8. To change the clock style on the Lock Screen, tap Lock Screen (see the picture below) and choose a clock. Then tap **Apply** to save the changes.

Tap "Lock Screen" to change the clock style on the lock screen

Tip: You can enable your phone to show you today's schedule and next alarm even when your screen is locked. To do this go to settings

> **Lock screen and security > Clock and FaceWidgets > FaceWidgets**. Then tap the status switches next to **Today's schedule** and **Next alarm.**

Fast Battery Charging

One of the cool features on Samsung Galaxy S9/S9 Plus is Fast Battery Charging. With this feature, your device can get 50% of battery power in about 40-50 minutes. You can learn how to use this feature by going to page 21.

Using the Edge Screen on Samsung Galaxy S9/S9 Plus

The Edge screen transforms the way you handle Samsung Galaxy S9/S9 Plus. Edge panels can be used to access apps, tasks, contacts and more. To access the Edge panel, drag the Edge panel handle located at the Edge of the screen. To access more Edge items, swipe again from the edge of the screen.

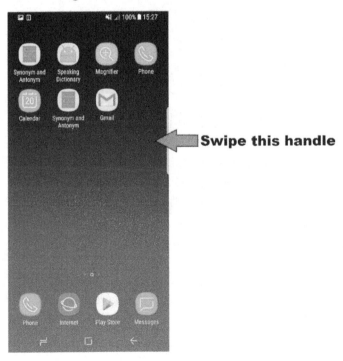

Swipe this handle

To access Edge panel settings, tap the settings  icon located at the bottom of the screen (this setting icon appears while viewing the Edge options).

Tip: You can view all the edge panels at once. To do this, drag the Edge panel handle located at the edge of the screen and then tap the menu icon. To access any of the panels displayed, simply tap it.

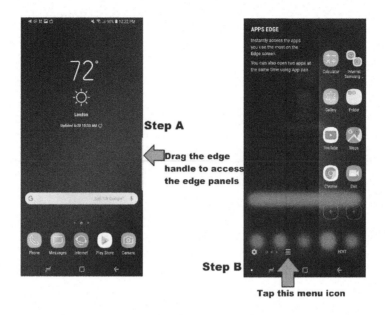

Using the Edge Panel

The Edge Panel allows you to use the Edge screen in a special way. To manage the Edge panel:

1. Swipe down from the top of the screen and select settings icon ⚙. Then tap **Display** tab.

2. Scroll down and tap **Edge Screen**.

3. Tap **Edge Panels**.

4. To download exciting panels, tap **Download** located at the top of the screen and tap the Edge panel you want to download. Then tap **Install** to download and install your chosen panel. To go back to the Edge panel screen, tap the back button ←.

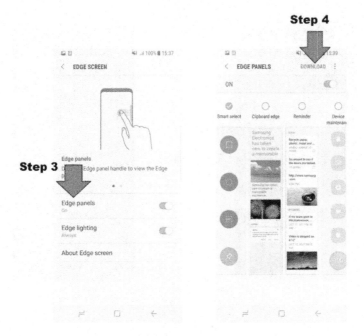

To see your newly installed panel, navigate to the **Edge Panels** screen and swipe left.

Swipe left to see the newly installed panel. In this case, calendar panel is the newly installed panel.

5. To uninstall an Edge panel that you don't like, tap the menu icon ⋮ located at the top of the Edge panel's screen and select **Uninstall**. Then select the minus icon (--) located at the top of the panel you want to uninstall. When prompted, tap **OK**. Please note that the uninstall button may not be available if you have not installed any Edge panel from the Edge panel store.

6. There are some Edge panels that allow you to edit them. To edit an editable panel, just tap **EDIT** next to the panel you want to edit. Please note that you may need to enable a panel before you can edit it. To learn how to enable a panel, please go to step 7.

Editable panel

Then tap and hold an item and move it to the Edge screen. To remove an item, tap the minus icon. To rearrange the icons, tap and drag the icon(s) to a new location. See the picture below.

Tap and drag any of these icons to move it to another location

Tap, hold and drag an icon to right side of the screen to add it to the edge screen

Tap this minus icon to remove an app from the edge screen

Although, *Apps Edge* has been used in the example above, you can also manage People Edge in similar way. In addition, please note that there is a maximum number of items you can add to the Edge screen.

To create "app pair" on the edge screen, tap **Create App pair**, select the two apps you like, and tap **DONE** to save the changes. To move the bottom app to top and vice versa, tap **Switch**. To delete your selection and select another apps, tap **Clear**.

7. To enable an Edge panel or select the Edge panel that you want to see on the Edge screen, simply tap/tick the circle on top of the panel. To disable/remove a panel, simply unselect the circle.

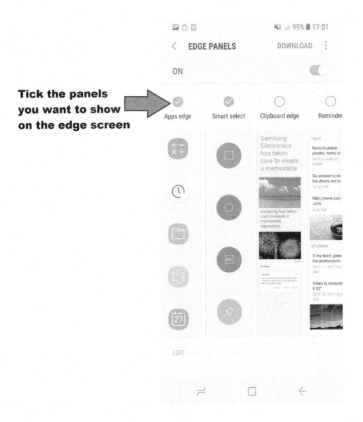

Tick the panels you want to show on the edge screen

8. To disable Edge panels, tap the status switch next to **ON**. Please note that when you disable Edge Panel, the Edge handle will disappear.

Note: If you download many Edge panels, you may not be able to access all these panels at once on your Edge screen. You may not be able to use more than nine Edge panels at once. To select the Edge panels that you want to access, simply follow the step 7 above.

Using the Edge Lighting

This feature allows you to set the Edge screen to light up when you receive calls or notifications.

1. Swipe down from the top of the screen and select settings

    icon 🔧 . Tap **Display** tab.
2. Scroll down and tap **Edge Screen**.

3. Tap **Edge Lighting**.

4. Tap the switch next to **ON**. The switch will appear bold when enabled.

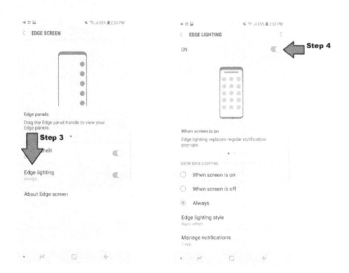

5. Select when to show the Edge lighting. If you want Edge Lighting to be active every time, then select **Always**.

6. Tap **Manage notifications** to select those apps that will work with Edge Lighting.

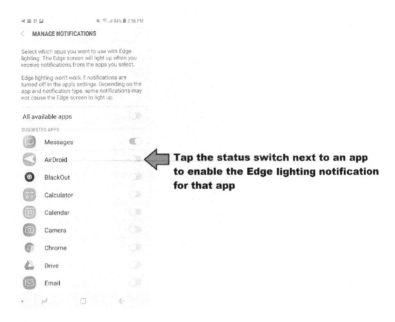

Select which apps you want to use with Edge lighting. The Edge screen will light up when you receive notifications from the apps you select.

Edge lighting won't work if notifications are turned off in the app's settings. Depending on the app and notification type, some notifications may not cause the Edge screen to light up.

All available apps

SUGGESTED APPS

Messages

AirDroid — **Tap the status switch next to an app to enable the Edge lighting notification for that app**

BlackOut

Calculator

Calendar

Camera

Chrome

Drive

Email

Note: It appears that not all notifications may be received as Edge lighting.

Tip: To customize the color, the size, or the transparency of the Edge lighting, tap the **Edge lighting style** and use the onscreen buttons to customize edge lighting. Then tap **Apply** to save the changes.

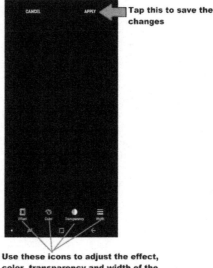

Tap this to save the changes

Use these icons to adjust the effect, color, transparency and width of the lighting

Reordering the Edge Screen Panel

1. Swipe down from the top of the screen and select settings icon 🔧 . Tap **Display** tab.

2. Scroll down and tap **Edge Screen**.

3. Tap **Edge Panels**.

4. Tap the menu ⋮ icon located at the top of the screen and tap **REORDER**.

5. Tap and hold the Re-order icon (◇) on an Edge screen panel and drag it to the desired position. Make sure that the panels

you use most are in the first 3 or 4 panels so that you can access them faster.

6. Tap back icon ← to save the changes.

Managing the Edge Panel Handle Settings/Changing the Edge Panel Location

Edge panel handle settings allows you to change the position of Edge panel and more.

1. Swipe down from the top of the screen and select settings icon ⚙. Tap **Display** tab.
2. Scroll down and tap **Edge Screen**.
3. Tap **Edge Panels**.
4. Tap the menu icon ⋮ located at the top of the screen and select **Edge panel handle.**
5. Under **Position** tab, tap the side you would like the panel to appear on.
6. To change the size of Edge panel, drag the slider next to **SIZE.**
7. To change the transparency of Edge panel, drag the slider next to **Transparency.**
8. To move the Edge panel handle to another part of the screen, tap and drag the Edge handle anchor (the small V-shape icon).

Drag this handle to move edge panel to another part of the screen

Using People Edge

People Edge gives you the opportunity to quickly access your favorite contacts from Edge Panel.

To manage People Edge:

1. Swipe down from the top of the screen and select settings icon ⚙. Tap **Display** tab.

2. Scroll down and tap **Edge Screen**.

3. Tap **Edge Panels**.

4. Tap **EDIT** under **People Edge.** If you can't see the Edit
    button, then People Edge is disabled. To enable People Edge,
    simply tap/tick the small circle ⭕ located on top of this
    panel.

5. Tap **SELECT CONTACT** and select all the contacts you
    want by tapping them. Please note that you may need to give
    access to People Edge before it can read your contacts. Tap
    DONE to save the changes. You should now be able to
    access the selected contacts when you access the Edge panel.

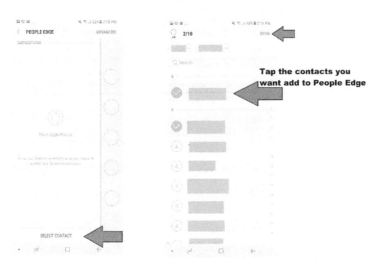

Tap the contacts you
want add to People Edge

6. To remove a contact from the People Edge, tap the minus
    icon next to the contact you want to remove.

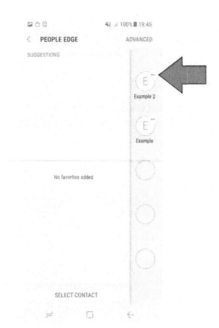

The Bixby

Bixby is a trained virtual assistant that has been built to answer questions, and let you interact with your phone in a special way. Bixby is divided into three parts:

1. Bixby Home
2. Bixby Vision
3. Bixby Voice

This section of the guide will show you how to manage Bixby like a pro.

Getting started with Bixby

You would need to setup Bixby when you first start using your device and you will learn how to do that in this section of the guide. To setup this voice assistant:

1. Press the Bixby button (the button next to volume button at the side of the phone).

2. If you see a screen telling you to update Bixby, simply tap **UPDATE.**

3. Tap **Next.**

4. Choose a language for Bixby Voice and tap **Confirm.**

5. Read the terms and conditions. If you agree to all the terms and conditions, tap **I have read and agreed to all** and then tap **NEXT.**

6. Follow the onscreen instructions to setup and register your voice so that Bixby can recognize your voice.

7. To manage a card, swipe in from the left edge of the screen and tap the menu icon ⋮ next to the card you want to manage. Then tap an option.

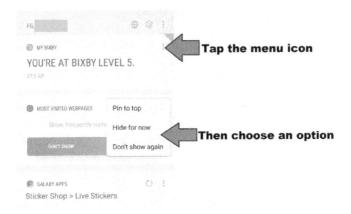

Tap the menu icon

Then choose an option

8. To adjust Bixby settings, tap the menu icon ⋮ located at top of the screen and tap **Settings**. Then choose an option.

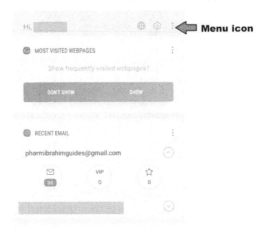

Menu icon

To choose which card is displayed to you on the Bixby home page; while on settings page, tap **Cards**, scroll down and use the status switch to turn off/on a card.

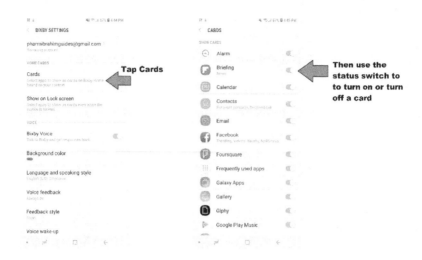

Tip: To customize the type of briefing you receive on the Bixby home page, tap the menu icon next to the briefing card and select **Customize content.**

Then choose the categories you want to receive information about.

Tap the back icon to save the changes.

Bixby Home

After the initial setup discussed above, you can access the Bixby Home by pressing the Bixby button (the button next to the volume button at the side of the phone). Alternatively, swipe right while on Home screen to access Bixby Home.

Bixby Voice

Bixby voice allows you to interact with Bixby using your voice.

Speaking to Bixby

One of the ways you will interact with Bixby is by speaking to it. The other way would be to type command into the search bar and hit **Go**.

To get Bixby into action, you would need to get its attention. To do that, perform any of the actions below:

1. Press the Bixby button located next to the volume button at the side of your phone and speak your command while still pressing it.

2. Alternatively, you can get Bixby's attention by saying **Hi Bixby!** However, you may need to enable this feature before you can put it to use. To enable **Hi Bixby** function:

- Press the dedicated Bixby button once (the button located next to the volume button at the side of the phone).

- Tap the menu icon ⋮ located at top of the screen and tap **Settings**.

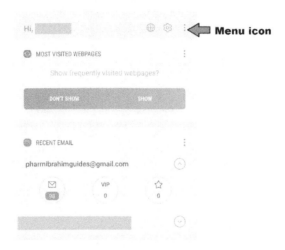

- Scroll down and tap **Voice wake-up.** Make sure the indicator switch under Voice Wake-Up is **ON** (see the picture below).

- If you want to increase the sensitivity of Bixby to the wake word, drag the slider under **Wake-up sensitivity** to medium or high position.

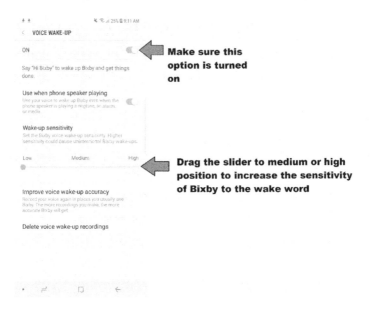

When Bixby is activated, it will respond by displaying a small action box on the screen. Bixby will then give you an answer to your request.

In addition, occasionally, you may notice that the question you asked Bixby is different from what it types into the action box. What Bixby types into the action box is what it thinks you have said.

Tip: You can train Bixby to better recognize your voice, to do this:

- Press the dedicated Bixby button once (the button located next to the volume button at the side of the phone).

- Tap the menu icon located at top of the screen and tap **Settings**.

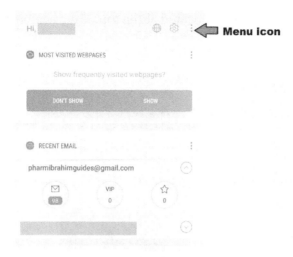

- Scroll down, tap **Enhanced voice recognition** and follow the onscreen instructions.

What about Typing?

The interesting thing is that Bixby can also listen when you command it using your onscreen keyboard. You can type in command and get a similar result just as you will get by speaking to it. This is a great feature especially if you can't speak to Bixby for one reason or the other e.g. if you are in a noisy place or your microphone is not working properly.

To use the Bixby typing feature:

- Press the Bixby button (located next to the volume button) for two to four seconds or say "**Hi Bixby**".
- Tap **Full Screen.**

- Tap the search bar located at the top of the screen and type your command.

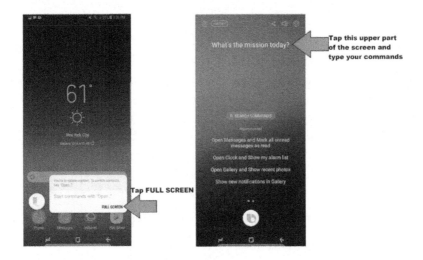

- Tap the send icon and wait for a reply.

Tip: If you are stuck and you don't know what to ask Bixby, you can use the typing menu to get some ideas. To do this, simply type a keyword into the search menu and scroll through the suggestions. For example, if you are searching for ideas on how to use Bixby with the Email app, just tap the text menu and key in **email**. Then scroll through the search results to see example commands.

Type a keyword and scroll through suggested commands.

Using Bixby to Open Apps or Programs

One of those things you will want to use Bixby to do is accessing your apps. You can quickly open an app by saying **Open** and then mention the name of the app. For example, to open settings, say or type **Open settings.** To open calculator, say **Open calculator**.

You may also say **Launch settings** instead of **Open settings.**

In addition, you may give a more specific command like **Open notification settings** to go to notification settings. Say **Launch Wi-Fi Settings** to open the Wi-Fi settings. To turn off airplane mode, say **Turn off airplane mode** and so on.

Using Bixby with Calendar

One of the fantastic features that Bixby can do for you is making an appointment. This personal assistant is built to work with your device Calendar making it easy for it to make appointments.

With just few commands, you can get Bixby to put an event or appointment into your Calendar. **To do this:**

1. Press the Bixby button located next to the volume button at the side of your phone and speak your command while still pressing it. Alternatively, say **Hi Bixby!**

2. Say whatever you want to include in the Calendar. For example, you can say any of the following:

   - Appointment with Clinton for Monday at 1 p.m.

   - Add meeting with Ibrahim at 10 a.m. on Sunday to my calendar.

   - Remind me to fix my car at 9 p.m. tonight. Please note that you can also say all the examples given above in other ways, the most important thing is to get Bixby to understand what you are saying.

   - When it has got the information, the Calendar/Reminder app will appear. You can then make any adjustment using the virtual keyboard.

Please note that when Do Not Disturb is running, you may not get voice feedback from Bixby, instead you may only get text feedback.

In addition, you can check how your calendar looks like. To do this, click the microphone button and say, "**What is on my calendar today?**" Or say, "**Any appointment today**?" Or just any variant. Note that you can also ask Bixby about your calendar for a day in the future. To do this, say "**Any appointment tomorrow?**" or say, "**Any appointment on November 1st?**"

Note: In case, Bixby sets a wrong appointment, you can edit it using your on-screen keyboard instead of trying to speak another word to it. Editing any misinformation with keyboard appears smarter and faster.

In addition, instead of speaking, you may type any of the commands mentioned above into the search box to get a similar result.

Using Bixby to Set Reminders

There are probably many things going through your mind, and it will be quite interesting if you can get a personal assistant to assist in remembering some of your duties. Fortunately, Bixby can help you in this regard.

To set a reminder using Bixby:

1. Press the Bixby button located next to the volume button at the side of your phone and speak your command while still pressing it. Alternatively, say **Hi Bixby!**

2. Say whatever you want to set a reminder for. For example, you can say the following:

   o Remind me to fix the car by 3 p.m.

   o Remind me to drop the meat pie at the restaurant.

   o Remind me to pick my daughter by 4 p.m.

   o Remind me to call Clinton at 1 p.m., and so on.

Please note that it is probably not compulsory that you put **remind** in every statement as I did above. But I would advise that you to do so whenever you can. This is because it will help Bixby to easily get what you are saying and avoid any confusion.

Note: In case, Bixby sets a wrong reminder, you can edit it using your on-screen keyboard instead of trying to speak another word to it. Editing any misinformation with keyboard appears smarter and faster.

Using Bixby with Alarm

You can also set an alarm using this personal assistant.

To do this:

1. Repeat the first step mentioned above.

2. Say the time for alarm. For example, you can say: "**set an alarm for 1 p.m. every Monday**" or "**alarm for 1 p.m. every Wednesday**" or "**set an everyday alarm for 2 p.m.**" or "**set an alarm for 1 p.m. on 24th of October**".

3. When it has grabbed the information, the alarm would appear, and it will tell you that it has set the alarm.

Using Bixby with Clock

You can ask Bixby what your local time is. In addition, it can also tell you the time in a specific place.

1. Press the Bixby button located next to the volume button at the side of your phone and speak your command while still pressing it. Alternatively, say **Hi Bixby!**

2. Then say, "**What is the time?**" or say, "**What is the time in New York?**"

Using Bixby to Get Flight Information

You can also use this virtual assistant to get information about a flight. This is a smarter way to know when an airplane will take off.

For example, you can say **Flight status of Delta 400** to get the information about this flight.

Using Bixby with Weather App

To know about the weather condition of a place, just say "**What's the weather going to be like today?**". You may also know about the weather condition of a place by asking "**What is the weather of New York today?**"

Using Bixby with Mail App

You can instruct Bixby to compose an email for you. To do this:

1. Press the Bixby button located next to the volume button at the side of your phone and speak your command while still pressing it. Alternatively, say **Hi Bixby!**

2. Then give the command. For example, you can say:

   - Send an email to Clinton.

   - Send an email to Clinton and Steve.

   - Search for emails from Clinton.

   - Search for emails from Steve and mark them all as important.

Please note that you will usually have to include one or more information before you send the email. Simply follow the voice prompts to add subject and email's body.

Tip: You can get example commands to help you use the email app like a pro. To do this, please refer to the **tip** on page 187.

Using Bixby with Map App

You can also use the Bixby to search the map. This virtual assistant is built to work with the Map app on your device. **To get how the map of a place looks like**:

1. Repeat the first step above.

2. Then say the map of an area you want to get. For example, you may say:

   - Map of Seattle.

   - Show me the map of Seattle.

What about Math?

Bixby can also help you with some mathematical calculations and conversions. For example, you can tell Bixby **What is the square root of four?** You can also say **convert one meter to centimeter**.

Using Bixby to Get Definitions

Also, you can ask Bixby for meaning of words. For example, you may say **what is the meaning of flabbergasted.**

Bixby's Settings

The settings tab allows you to manage Bixby's functions. To access Bixby's settings:

1. Press the dedicated Bixby button once (the button located next to the volume button at the side of the phone).

2. Tap the menu icon ⋮ located at top of the screen and tap **Settings**.

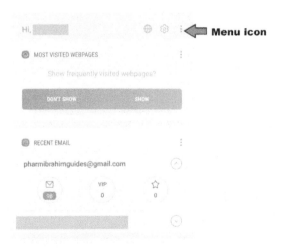

3. Tap an option.

The settings menu allows you to manage Bixby like a maven. I would advise that you take time to go through the various settings options on the settings page.

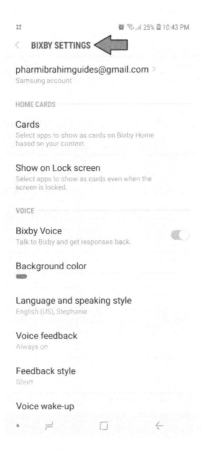

How to Clear Bixby's Voice Interaction Data

To erase whatever voice interaction Bixby has stored:

4. Press the dedicated Bixby button once (the button located next to the volume button at the side of the phone).

5. Tap the menu icon ⋮ located at the topmost part of the screen and tap **Settings**.

6. Scroll down and tap **Privacy.**

7. Tap **Erase Bixby Voice interaction data.**

Troubleshooting Bixby

Although much efforts have been put into making this virtual assistant, I am quite sure that Bixby will misbehave at one time or the other. When this happens, there are few things to do.

- **Ensure that you are connected to a strong network**: If you have a bad or no internet connection, Bixby may not work properly. Therefore, the first thing to check when Bixby starts to misbehave is the internet connection.

- **Use the Virtual Keyboard**: You may need to use the keyboard to pass your message to Bixby if you find out that it is not getting your speech. Many of what you say (If not all) can also be typed into the Bixby's search bar. Please go to page 185 to learn more about this.

- **Try to Restart Your Phone**: If you find out that what I have mentioned above do not work, try restarting your phone.

Conclusion

Bixby is like a learning machine and it is being improved upon. If you are having difficulty passing your message across to it, you may try typing some of your commands into the command box (see page 185). I strongly believe you will know how to use it more as time goes on.

Bixby Vision

Bixby allows you to interact with images in an educating manner. It also gives you more understanding of what you are looking at. When first using Bixby Vision, you may need to agree to some terms and conditions.

To Use Bixby Vision:

1. Launch the camera app of your phone.
2. Aim the lens of the camera at what you want to capture.
3. Tap the Bixby button. You can use the Bixby Vision to extract texts, translate a language, scan Barcodes, shop etc.

Bixby vision icon

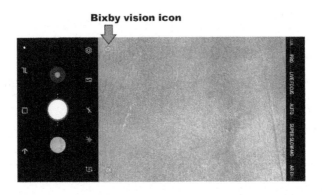

4. Choose an option. For example, if you are trying to extract a text, scroll right or left and tap **Text**. Then tap **Text** again to extract the texts.

5. To exit, tap the back button ←.

You can also access Bixby vision while using the Gallery app. Simply launch the **Gallery** app, tap an image and tap the Bixby button. Please note that some pictures may not have Bixby button.

Bixby button

Using the Web

Internet App

Opening the Internet Browser

The first thing you would need to do to use the Internet app is to open it. To do this:

1. From the Home screen, tap **Internet** .

2. Alternatively, go to the app screen by swiping up from the bottom of the screen and tap **Samsung** folder. Tap **Internet** .

3. If you are using the Internet app for the first time, follow the prompts to get started.

Get to Know the Internet Browser Interface

When you open the Internet app, you should see the following buttons/icons:

1	**Favorite:** Tap this icon to bookmark a webpage.
2	**Refresh:** Tapping this icon reloads a webpage.
3	**Menu icon:** Tap this icon to access additional options such as **Find on page** and **save webpage** etc.
4	**Tabs:** Tap this to navigate between different webpages. Tap and hold the tab icon to quickly open your browser's home page.

5	**Bookmarks:** Tap this icon to access bookmark pages, saved pages and history.
6	**Home:** Tap this icon to go to the browser's home page. To quickly change the default Homepage, tap and hold the Home icon and then select **Other.** Then enter the website of your choice (e.g. bing.com) and tap **OK.**
7	**Forward**: Tap this icon to return to the page you just left.
8	**Back:** Tap this icon to revisit the page you just visited. To quickly access browsing history, tap and hold the back button $<$
9	**Quick Menu:** Tap this button to access the quick menu. Quick menu allows you to quickly share a webpage, increase webpage font, or open a new tab. To move this icon to another location, simply tap, hold and drag the icon to the new location. To remove the icon; tap, hold and drag it to the top of the screen (where Remove icon is located).

Customizing the Home Page

The Home page is the page that opens when you open your Internet browser. Fortunately, you can choose what appears on your home page.

To do this:

- While the Internet browser is opened, tap menu icon 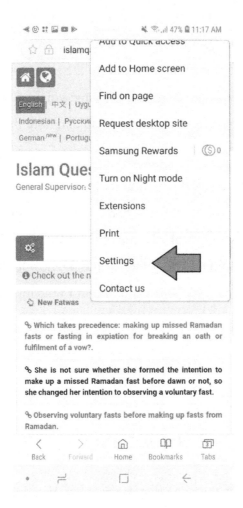 and then scroll down and tap on **Settings.**

- Tap **Home page** and then choose an option.

- To go to the Home page while using your internet browser, tap the internet browser Home button ⌂ .

Tip: To quickly change the default Homepage, tap and hold the Home icon ⌂ and then select an option.

Using the Address/Search Bar

Every web browser must have an address bar and Internet browser also has one. This bar serves the function of URL address bar and search bar. By default, the searches done on this bar is executed by Google. To learn how to change the search engine to another one, please go to page 213.

You choose whether to launch a webpage or search for a term based on what you type into the address bar. For example, if you type **Freedom to** into the address bar and tap **Go**, Google search results for that phrase is displayed. On the other hand, if you type **Freedom.to** and tap **Go**, you will be taken to the website bearing the name.

Internet browser makes website suggestions to you based on the sites you have recently visited, to choose any of this suggested site, tap it.

When you begin to type inside the address bar, Internet browser automatically makes suggestions beneath your typing. You can choose any of these suggestions to make things faster.

Zooming a Webpage in Internet Browser

To zoom in a webpage in Internet browser, place two fingers on the webpage and spread them apart. To zoom out, place two fingers on the webpage and move them closer together. To force zoom a webpage that doesn't readily respond to a zoom request, turn on the **Manual zoom.** To do this, while the Internet browser is opened, tap

menu icon ⋮ located at the top of the screen and then scroll down and tap on **Settings**. Tap the status switch next to **Manual Zoom.**

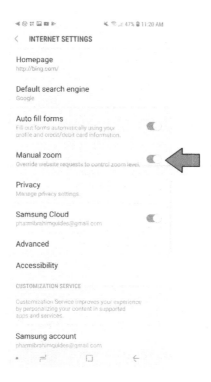

Using Tabs on Internet Browser

The tabs allow you to open different webpages at once. You can open many tabs at once on Internet browser.

To manage browsing tabs:

1. Tap the tab icon ⬚ located at the bottom of the screen.
2. To open a new tab, tap **New Tab**.

3. To access a tab you have opened before, tap the tab icon  and then tap your desired tab.

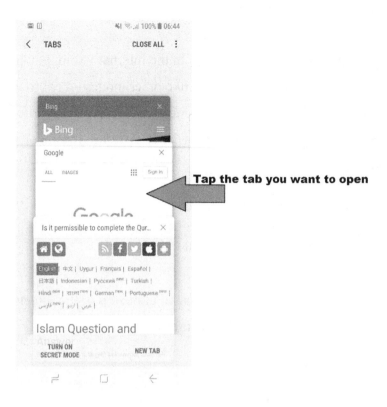

Tap the tab you want to open

4. To close a tab, tap the **X** icon at the top right corner of the thumbnail of the tab you want to close.

5. To close all tabs, while on the tabs' screen, tap **CLOSE ALL** located at the top of the screen.

Favorites (Bookmarks)

With several billions of webpages in the internet world, you just have to select your favorites. Just like other modern-day browsers, Internet browser gives you the opportunity to select a favorite or bookmark a page. This makes it easier to visit the website or webpage in the future.

To bookmark a webpage:

1. Open the website you want to bookmark.

2. Tap the menu icon ⋮ located at the top of the screen and then select **Add to Bookmarks**.

3. Key in the **Title** you want.

4. Tap **Save.**

Tip: To quickly add a bookmark, just open the webpage and tap

favorite icon next to the address bar.

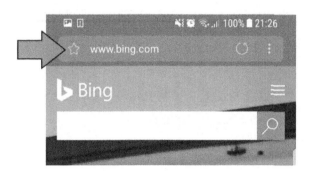

Accessing Your Bookmarks/Favorites

After you have added a webpage to your favorites list, you will need

to access this list sooner or later. To access your bookmarks, tap the

Bookmark icon (located at the bottom of the screen).

Saving a Webpage

Webpages contain a lot of information and you would probably need to schedule some webpages for later reading. Saving a webpage is a great way to do this. When you find an interesting information online and you don't have the time to read it, you can save it for a later reading.

To save a webpage, open the webpage and tap ⋮ (next to address bar) and then select **Save webpage**.

Accessing Your Saved Pages

After you have saved a page, you would need to access this page sooner or later. To do this, tap the **Bookmarks** icon (located at the bottom of the screen) and then tap **Saved Pages** located at the top of the screen.

Changing the Search Engine

The default search engine on Internet browser is Google. Some people may love to change this to another search engine.

You can change the Internet browser Search Engine by following the steps highlighted below:

1. While the browser is opened, tap menu icon ⋮ (next to address bar) and select **Settings**.

2. Tap on **Default search engine** and select a search engine.

Making Internet App Your Default Browser

If you have multiple browsers on your device, you can select internet app to be the default browser. To do this:

1. Swipe down from the top of the screen and select settings icon ⚙.

2. Tap **Apps** and then tap the menu icon ⋮ .
3. Tap **Default apps**.
4. Tap **Browser app** and choose **Samsung Internet**.

Hint: You can use the method mentioned above to set other favorite app(s) as default app(s). For example, if you have many Contact apps on your device, you can select a default Contact app using this method.

Managing the History List

If the secret mode is not enabled, Internet browser collects the history of the webpages you visit and stores it.

To access your history:

1. Tap the **Bookmarks** ⬚⬚ (located at the bottom of the screen).

2. Tap **History**.

Hint: To clear the browsing data, tap ⋮ (located at the top of the screen) > **Settings** > **Privacy** > **Delete personal data.** Select what you would like to delete, and tap **Delete.**

In addition, if you see that a website/webpage is misbehaving, you can try deleting the *cache, cookies and site data,* and see if this would solve the problem. To do this, tap ⋮ (located at the top of the screen) > **Settings** > **Privacy** > **Delete personal data.** Select **Cache, Cookies and site data** and then tap **Delete**.

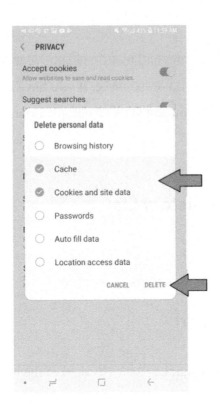

Sharing a Webpage with Friends

To share a webpage with friends, open the Internet app and tap the

menu icon ⋮ next to the address bar. Then tap on **Share**. Then

choose an app and follow the prompts.

Add Your Favorite Webpage to the Home Screen

You can make your favorite webpage a shortcut on the Home screen. This allows you to easily access the webpage directly from your Home screen. To do this:

1. Open a webpage and tap on the menu icon ⋮ (next to the address bar).

2. Tap **Add shortcut on Home screen**.

3. Tap **Add.**

4. To see the newly added webpage, tap the home button □ (located at the bottom of the screen). If you can't see it on the first home screen, swipe left to check another home screen.

Printing Web Pages on the Internet browser

Printing on the Internet browser is quite fantastic. You can initiate the printing process by tapping on the menu icon (the three dots icon located next to the address bar). Then tap **Print.** Tap the **dropdown arrow** to select a printer. To adjust the printing options, tap **Copies**.

To save the webpage as a pdf, tap the dropdown arrow and select

Save as PDF. Thereafter, tap the yellow **PDF** icon and choose a folder. Then tap **Done** to download.

Tap this to adjust the printing options

The dropdown arrow

Secret Mode

There are times when you will not want your browser to save any information about your visit to a webpage. For instance, if you don't want a website to save cookies on your device or you don't want your children to know you are browsing about favorite gifts to buy for them.

In addition, Secret mode browsing allows for multiple sessions. For example, you may access your Yahoo mail account (or another web account) on a normal window and use the Secret mode tab to open the Yahoo mail account of that of your friend or family member without logging out of your account. Pages viewed in secret mode are not listed in your browser history or search history, and leave no traces (such as cookies) on your device.

To activate the Secret mode, in the toolbar at the bottom of the screen, tap **Tabs** → **Turn on Secret mode.**
Then tap **Set password** to protect your Secret mode data with a password. You may also tap **Do not use password** if you don't want to use a password.

To deactivate the Secret mode, close the Internet app. Alternatively, tap the tab button , tap **Close All** (located at the top of the screen) and then select **Turn Off Secret Mode.**

More on Internet browser Settings

Many options under settings have already been discussed, but there are still some that I would like to mention.

1. **Auto fill profile:** Use this option to enable Internet browser to save your form entries whenever you fill in information

into an online form so that it can be used when you are filling similar forms in the future.

2. **Privacy**: Use this option to access settings such as **cookies**, **personal data** and so on. You can use the privacy tab to delete history information on your browser. To do this, tap **Delete personal data**.

3. **Advanced**: Use this option to access advanced options like **JavaScript**, **Pop-up blocker**, **Status bar**, **Manage website data** and **Web notifications**.

4. **Accessibility**: You can manage *high contrast mode* under this tab.

5. **Samsung account**: This tab displays the Samsung account address on your mobile phone.

6. **Personal information**: Use this tab to manage those information that can be sent to Samsung in order to provide you a customized experience.

7. **About Samsung Internet:** Use this option to get software information about the Internet app.

More on the Menu Icon

Many options under the **menu** tab ⋮ have already been discussed, but I will still like to point out few more things.

1. **Add to Quick access**: Use this option to add a webpage to your quick access list so that you can access it easily in the future from the internet app homepage. To make sure you go to Quick access page when you tap the Internet browser home button 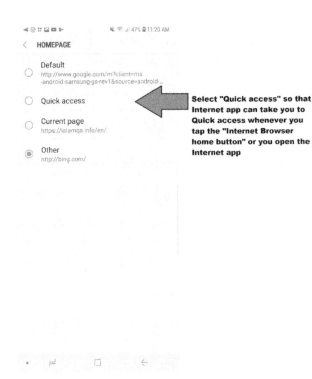, tap and hold Internet browser home button and select Quick access.

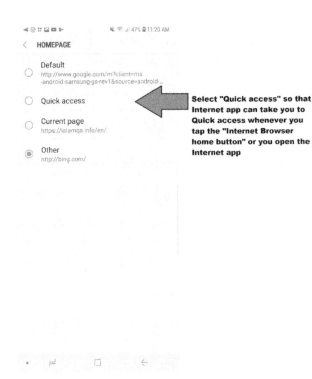

2. **Add to Home screen:** Use this option to make a webpage a shortcut on your Home screen.

3. **Find on page:** Use this option to search for a word or a phrase on a webpage.

4. **Request desktop site:** Use this option to request the desktop version of a webpage.

5. **Turn on Night mode:** Use this option to give a webpage a darkish background.

6. **Extensions:** Internet app browser's extensions allow you to do more when using the Internet app. To see which extensions are available on Internet app, tap **Extensions.**

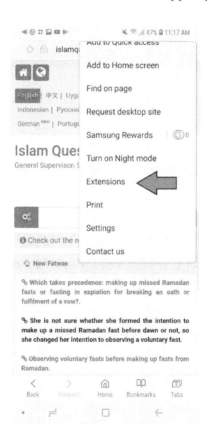

Troubleshooting the Internet browser

Internet browser may sometimes refuse to work properly, or it may hang. If this happens, just close the browser and open it again. To close the Internet app, tap the recent button (located at the bottom of the screen) to view all the opened apps and then tap **X** next to the Internet app thumbnail. If the browser refuses to close, try restarting your phone.

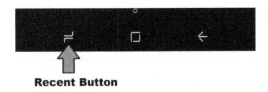

Recent Button

In addition, if you see that a website/webpage is misbehaving, you can try deleting the *cache, cookies and site data* and see if this would solve the problem. To do this, tap Internet app menu icon

⋮ (located at the top of the screen) > **Settings** > **Privacy** > **Delete personal data.** Select **Cache, Cookies and site data** and then tap **Delete**.

Troubleshooting Internet Connection when Using the Internet Browser

Internet browser may sometimes refuse to browse the internet. When this happens, you may try any of the suggestions below:

1. Check if you are connected to a wireless network. When Wi-Fi is connected, active, and it is communicating with a wireless Access Point, **Wi-Fi active icon** is displayed on the status bar at the top of the screen. If your phone is not connected to a network, swipe down from the top of the

screen and tap **settings icon** 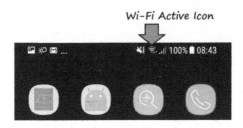 > **Connections**. Tap **Wi-Fi**, and then tap On/Off to turn Wi-Fi on.

Wi-Fi Active Icon

2. If you are trying to use a cellular connection and not a Wi-Fi connection, then check your cellular data connection. Swipe down from the top of the screen, tap the **settings icon** > **Connections >Data Usage**. Then make sure the switch next to **Mobile data** is turned on.

3. If you are trying to roam while abroad, check that you have allowed roaming. Swipe down from the top of the screen and tap the **settings icon** > **Connections** > **Mobile networks** > **Data Roaming**. Then make sure the switch next to **Data Roaming** is switched on. Please note that when roaming, international roaming charges may apply.

If after trying all the options above, and you can't still browse, then make sure that you have not mistakenly/knowingly installed a new browsing setting on your phone. If you have installed new settings from a text message, then uninstall the new settings. To do this, swipe down from the top of the screen and tap the **settings icon**

⚙ > **Apps**. Look for the new settings. Tap the new settings and tap **Uninstall**.

Communication

Calling

Learn how to use the calling functions, such as making and answering calls, using options available during a call, and using call-related features.

Making, Answering, Rejecting and Silencing a Call

To make a call or silence a call:

1. While on the home screen, tap **Phone** and enter a phone number. If the keypad does not appear on the screen, tap the keypad button to show the keypad. To call a number on your contact, tap the **Contact** button on the Phone app screen.

2. To make a call from the **Recents** tab, tap the **Recents** tab located at the top of the screen.

3. To make a phone call, tap a contact and then tap the phone icon .

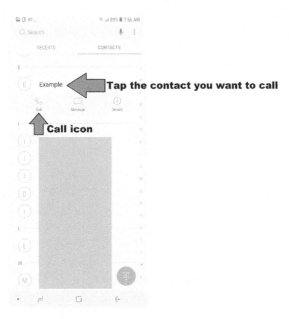

4. To silence or reduce the volume of an incoming call, press the volume down button (located at the side of the phone).

Hint: You can access apps/items on your phone while receiving a call. To do this, tap the home key located at the lower side of the screen and tap the item/app you want to access.

Tip: To call the contact whose message or contact details are currently on the screen, bring the phone close to your ear. However, please note that you may need to enable this option. To do this, swipe down from the top of the screen and tap the **settings icon** > **Advanced features.** Then tap the status switch next to **Direct call**.

To answer a call or reject an incoming call:

1. To receive an incoming call, tap or drag the **Green phone icon** .

2. To decline an incoming call, tap or drag the **Red phone icon** .

3. To reply with a text, swipe up from the bottom of the screen or tap **Send Message.**

Swipe up to reply with a message

4. Then tap one of the pre-written messages. Alternatively, tap **Compose new message**, and write your message.

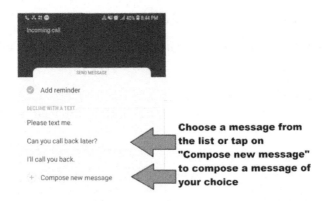

Choose a message from the list or tap on "Compose new message" to compose a message of your choice

Hint: If you are using an app, a pop-up screen is displayed for the incoming call, just tap the corresponding icon to accept, decline the call or reply with a message.

In addition, you can create rejection messages of your own. From the Home screen, tap **Phone** > **Menu icon** ⋮ > **Settings** > **Quick decline message** , enter a message, and then tap **Plus icon +.** To delete a message, tap the minus icon next to it.

If a phone number calls you or you call a number and you don't have it on your contact, you can easily add it to your contact. To do this, tap **Phone** app and tap **Recents.** Then tap the contact and tap **Details.** Tap **Create Contact** (located at the bottom of the screen) and follow the prompts.

Tip: To quickly reject an incoming call with a preset rejection message, place your finger on the heart rate monitor for two seconds while the phone screen is facing down. The heart rate monitor is located under the flash light at the back of your phone. *Please note that this option may only work when your device is turned over and the screen is off.*

You can edit the preset rejection message. To do this:

1. Swipe down from the top of the screen and select settings icon ⚙ . Tap **Display** tab.

2. Scroll down and tap **Edge Screen**.

3. Tap **Edge Lighting**.

4. Tap the menu icon ⋮ located at the top of the screen.

5. Tap **Quick reply**.

6. Type in a **Quick Reply Message** and tap the back icon next to QUICK REPLY to save the changes.

Learn How to Use Your Phone During a Call

You can perform any of these tasks when on a call:

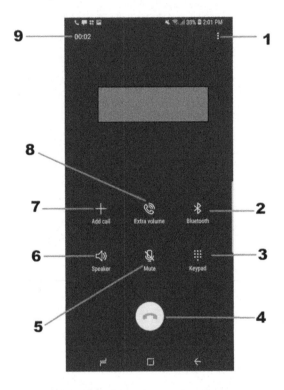

Number	Function
1.	Tap the **Menu icon** to hold a current call, view a contact or add a number to contact, or send a message.
2.	Tap the Bluetooth icon to connect to a Bluetooth headset while on a call.
3.	Tap the keypad icon to access the keypad. To hide the keypad, tap the **Hide** icon.
4.	Tap the red phone icon to **end a call**.

5.	Tap this icon to mute the microphone.
6.	To turn Speakerphone on or off, tap the speaker icon.
7.	Tap the plus icon to add another contact to a call or start another call.
8.	Tap extra volume icon to add extra volume to a call.
9.	Call time

Tip: To access the application screen while on a call, tap the Home button. If you want to return to the call screen, swipe down from the top of the screen and tap the current call.

Place a New Call While on a Call (Conference Calling)

If your network service provider supports this feature, you can make another call while a call is in progress.

1. From the active call screen, tap + **Add call**.

2. Dial the new number and tap 📞 **Dial**. When the call is answered:

   i.   Tap 🔁 **Swap** to switch between the two calls.

ii.   Tap  **Merge** to turn the call to a conference call.

3. To end a call while on a conference call mode, tap the dropdown arrow (next to **Conference call**) and then select **Drop** next to the call you want to end.

Emergency Calling

You can use Samsung Galaxy S9/S9 Plus to make an emergency call. From the Home screen, tap **Phone** icon and enter the emergency telephone number. Note that if you dial 911 in the U.S, your location details may be provided to an emergency service provider even if your settings does not support this.

Please note that an emergency number can be dialed even if the phone is locked.

Using Call Waiting

Call waiting allows you to get another call while you're already in one.

1. To answer the new call, drag **Answer** to the right direction and then choose an option:

    i.   **Put ...on hold** to place the previous caller on hold while you answer the new call.

    ii. **End call with...** to end the previous call and answer the new call.

2. Once the other call is answered, tap the swap icon next to the contact or phone number you wish to continue talking to. The other(s) would be put on hold. To merge the calls, tap merge icon .

Please note that call waiting may be disabled by default. To enable this feature, tap **Phone** > **Menu icon** > **Settings** > **More settings,** and then tap the switch next to **Call waiting.**

Using the Speed Dial Options

The speed dial allows you to quickly access a number in your contact. To set up speed dial:

1. Tap the phone icon

2. Tap **Contacts** located at the top of the screen.

3. Tap **menu icon** located at the top of the screen.

4. Tap **Speed dial**.

5. To add a contact to the speed dial, tap the contact icon Ⓡ .

6. To change the speed dial number, tap the dropdown arrow and pick a number. Number one is reserved for voicemail.

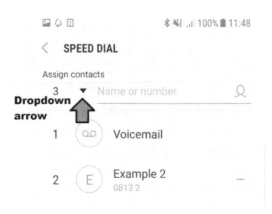

7. To call a contact you have added, tap the phone app icon and from the dial pad, press and hold the number assigned to the desired contact. To call a contact assigned to a two-digit speed dial, dial the first number, then press and hold the 2nd number.

8. To delete a speed dial number, tap the **Minus (-)** icon next to the assigned contact. Removing a contact from a speed dial list will not delete it from your phone.

Using the Fixed Dialing Option

If you want to select the numbers your mobile phone can call, you need to turn on the fixed dialing. Once done, you can only call the selected numbers and emergency numbers.

1. From the Home screen, tap **PHONE app icon** .

2. Tap **menu icon** located at the top of the screen.

3. Tap **Settings**.

4. Scroll down and tap **More settings**.

5. Tap **Fixed Dialing Numbers**.

6. To turn the fixed dialing on, tap **Turn on FDN**, type in your **PIN2** and tap **OK**. Please contact your local network service provider for your PIN2.

7. To turn the fixed dialing off, tap **Turn off FDN**, enter your **PIN2** and tap OK. Please contact your local network service provider for your PIN2.

Note: I am not sure if all network providers support this feature. If you notice that this feature is not available on your phone, you may need to contact your service provider to know if you can use this feature.

Adding Fixed Dialing Numbers

1. Repeat the steps 1 to 5 above.

2. Tap **FDN List**.

3. Tap **ADD** located at the top of the screen.

4. Tap **Name** and enter the required name.

5. Tap **NUMBER** and enter the required phone number.

6. Tap **PIN2** and enter the PIN2. Please contact your local network service provider for your PIN2.

7. Tap **SAVE** located at the top of the screen.

Please note that when FDN is enabled, you may not be able to call any other numbers, apart from the numbers on the FDN list and the emergency numbers.

Call Forwarding (Diverting Calls to Another Number)

When you are busy, you can forward incoming calls to another phone number. Please note that your network provider would need to support this feature for it to be available.

1. From the Home screen, tap **PHONE app icon** .

2. Tap **menu icon** located at the top of the screen.

3. Tap **Settings**.

4. Scroll down and tap **More settings**.

5. Tap **Call forwarding**.

6. Tap the required divert type and follow the onscreen instructions. For example, to forward all your calls, tap **Always forward**.

7. To turn off call forwarding, select a divert type and select **turn off.**

Note: When the call forwarding option is enable, you should see the call forwarding icon (see the picture below) on the notification bar at the top of the screen.

In addition, depending on your network provider, you may be able to forward calls to your voice mail and listen to them later.

Block Calls

If your service provider supports this feature, you may be able to avoid receiving calls from certain numbers. Please note that the call blocking feature may not affect phone calls made or received via apps (e.g. Skype) installed on your device.

Please note that features available under Call blocking may differ from one service provider to another.

1. From the Home screen, tap **PHONE app icon** .

2. Tap **menu icon** located at the top of the screen.

3. Tap **Settings**.

4. Tap **Block numbers**.

5. To add a number to your block list, enter the desired phone number in the **Add phone number** field, then tap the + icon. To add a number from your contacts, tap Contacts icon

   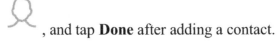, and tap **Done** after adding a contact.

6. To remove a number from your block list, tap the Minus (-) icon next to a name or number on your block list.

7. To make sure that only the numbers that you have their contacts can call you, tap the status switch next to **Block unknown callers**.

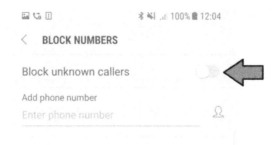

Note: In certain instances, blocking anonymous call may be unbeneficial and even dangerous. For example, blocking anonymous call may prevent you from accepting calls from those who have something important to tell you (unless you have their contacts). *In addition, if you are not able to use call blocking option after following the instructions above, please contact your network service provider.*

Tip: To block a contact from call log, follow these steps:

1. From the Home screen, tap **PHONE app icon** .

2. Tap **Recents** (located at the top of the screen).

3. Tap the contact you want to block and tap details icon ⓘ.

4. Tap **menu icon** ⋮ located at the top of the screen.

5. Tap **Block contact.**

*If you don't have the number that you want to block on your contact, repeat steps 1 to 3 above and then tap **Block number** located at the bottom of the screen.*

What about Caller ID?

If your service provider supports this feature, you may prevent your service provider from displaying your number(ID) when you call another person.

1. From the Home screen, tap **PHONE app icon** .

2. Tap **menu icon** located at the top of the screen.

3. Tap **Settings**.

4. Scroll down and tap **More settings**.

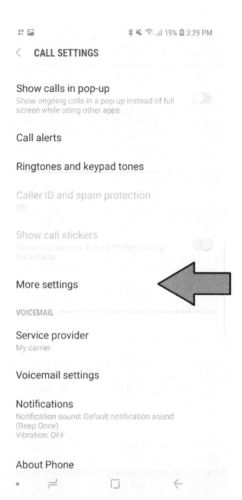

Show calls in pop-up
Show ongoing calls in a pop-up instead of full
screen while using other apps.

Call alerts

Ringtones and keypad tones

Caller ID and spam protection
Off

Show call stickers
To use call stickers, turn on Profile sharing
in Contacts.

More settings

VOICEMAIL

Service provider
My carrier

Voicemail settings

Notifications
Notification sound: Default notification sound
(Beep Once)
Vibration: OFF

About Phone

5. Tap **Show my caller ID** and then choose an option.

Using the Messaging app

This app allows you to send texts, images, and video messages to other SMS and MMS devices.

To start or manage a conversation:

1. Tap the **Messages** app icon from Home screen.

2. Tap the new message icon located at the bottom right corner of the screen.

3. Type in the first letters of the recipient's name. The list filters as you type. Then tap the required contact. Note; depending on your service provider, you can add up to 20 contacts (if not more). If you don't have the number on your contact, just key in the number in **Search Contacts or enter number field**. To remove a contact from the send list, just tap the minus icon (-) next to the contact.

4. Tap the **Start** icon located at the top of the screen and write the text for your SMS/MMS.

5. To attach a file such as audio, tap the plus icon and then tap the menu icon (the three dots icon) and choose an option.

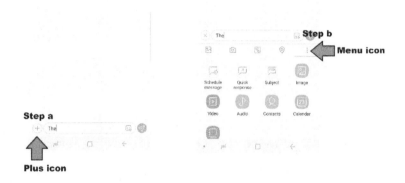

6. When you are done, tap Send icon . If prompted, tap **Send**.

7. To reply a message, tap the message and then enter a

message in the reply field. Tap Send icon when you are done.

8. To **Delete** a conversation, press and hold the message in question and tap on **Delete.**

9. In a conversation, you can press and hold a message to **forward, copy, share** or **delete** the message.

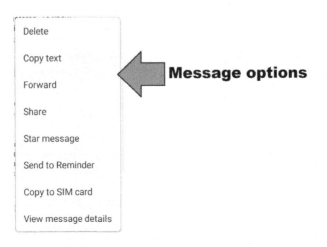

Delete

Copy text

Forward

Share

Star message

Send to Reminder

Copy to SIM card

View message details

Message options

Hints:

- If you receive an attachment, you can tap on the attachment to view it. To save an attachment, tap and hold the attachment and select **save attachment**. You can also tap the **Share** icon to share the attachment. To view saved attachments, go to the app screen, tap **Samsung** folder, tap **My files** and then tap a content category. Alternatively, visit **Photos/Gallery** app if the attachment is an image.

- To customize your message settings, from the message screen, tap menu icon ⋮ and select **Settings.** Tap the desired setting to adjust. To access more settings, tap **More Settings.** *Please note that the features available on message settings may differ from one service provider to another.*

‹ SETTINGS

| Notifications |
| Block numbers and messages |
| More settings |
| Emergency alert settings |
| Privacy |
| About Messages |

Message settings menu

- **You can block text messages** from certain numbers, if your service provider supports this feature. To do this, Tap the menu icon ⋮ > **Settings** > **Block numbers and messages** > **Block numbers**. Then enter the desired number in the **Enter number** field and tap the + icon to add the entered number to the message block list. To go into your contacts/ message inbox, tap **Contacts/Inbox**. To remove a number from the message block list, tap the minus (-) icon.

- When you receive a message, you can easily save the number if it is not yet saved in your contacts. To do this, tap the messaging app. Tap a conversation, tap the menu icon ⋮ located at the top right corner of the screen and tap the number in question. Thereafter, tap **Create contact** (located at the bottom of the screen). Follow the on-screen instructions to finish the process.

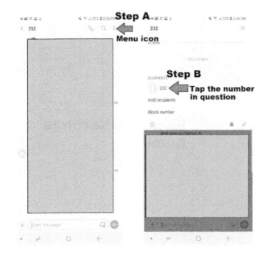

Step A

Menu icon

Step B

Tap the number in question

Step C

EMAIL APP

Introduction

Samsung Galaxy S9/S9 Plus comes preloaded with an email app for sending and receiving emails. One of the things you will need to do when you start using this device is to set up an email account. In this section of the guide, I will be discussing how to use your mail app like a maven.

How to Add Your Email Accounts to the Email app

You may probably have many email accounts and you may wish to add these accounts to the email app on your device.

The email accounts you can add to the Mail app include Google Mail, Yahoo Mail, iCloud, Exchange, Outlook among others.

To add an email account:

1. Swipe down from the top of the screen and select settings icon ⚙.

2. Tap **Cloud and accounts**.

3. Tap **Account.**

4. Tap **Add account.**

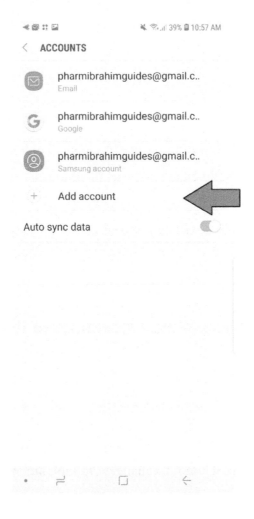

5. Tap **Email** and fill in the details.

6. To add another email account, repeats steps 1 to 5 above.

7. To add an Exchange account, select **Exchange** and follow the prompts. In addition, to add a Google account, tap **Google** and follow the prompts.

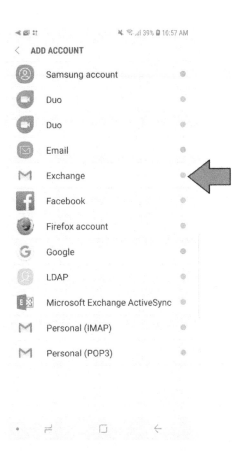

Special Note on Adding Exchange Account to the Email App

Following the instructions above might not be enough when you want to add your Exchange account to the Email app and you may need an extra information. You may need to obtain from your Exchange administrator or provider the account's server address, domain name, and username in addition to your email address and password.

How to Compose and Send an Email Message Using the Email App

You can easily send an email message to your friends or organization using the Email App. In this section of the guide, we will be exploring how to compose and send an email message.

To send an email message:

- From the Home screen, swipe up and tap **Email** . If you can't see the Email app, check **Samsung** folder on the application screen.

- To change to another email account if multiple email accounts are configured, swipe right from the left edge of the screen and tap an account.

- To compose a new email, tap the new email icon located at the bottom of the screen.

- Tap the field next to **To** and type in the email address of the recipient. You can also tap the contact icon to view and add contacts.

- To send a copy to another person, tap the dropdown icon ⌄ next to **To** and type the person's email address in the **Cc/Bcc** field.

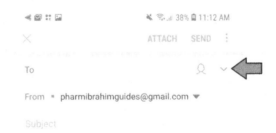

Tip: Cc means Carbon Copy. If you use the Cc option to send a message to many recipients, all the recipients will see the message and all other email addresses that have received the message. On the other hand, Bcc stands for Blind Carbon Copy. If you use Bcc option to send a message to many recipients, all the recipients will see the message, but will not see other email addresses that have received the message.

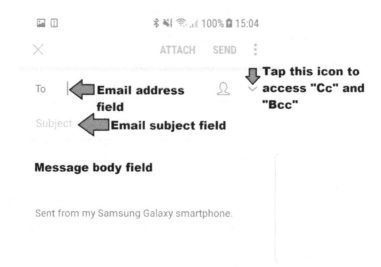

- If you have more than one email account configured on Mail app and you wish to send from a different email account, tap the dropdown icon next to **From** to choose a different email account. See the picture below.

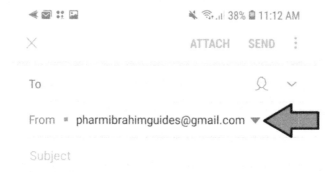

- Tap **Subject** field and key in the subject of your email.
- Tap the text input field and write the text for your email.

- You can use the formatting tab at the bottom of the screen to perform the following actions:

1. **Undo:** Tap to undo an action.

2. **Redo:** Tap to redo an action.

3. **Image:** Tap this to add an image.

4. **Font:** Tap this to change the font type.

5. **Font Size**: Use this option to change the font size of your text.

6. **Bold**: You can bold a part or your entire message using this feature. To bold a text, select the text(s) and tap the **B** icon.

7. **Italicize**: You can make your text appear italicized by clicking on the *I* icon.

8. **Underline**: Use the U icon to underline a text.

9. **Font color**: Tap this to change the font color.

10. **Font background color**: Tap this to change the font background color.

11. **Numbering**: Tap this to create a numbered list.

12. **Bullets**: Tap this to create a bullet list.

13. **Increase indent**: Tap this to move the paragraph farther away from the margin.

14. **Decrease indent**: Tap this to move the paragraph towards the margin.

To access more formatting options, swipe the formatting icons to the left or right. (See the arrows below).

1. When you are satisfied with the message and you are ready to send it, tap **Send** located at the top of the Email app screen.

Note: Before you can apply some of the formatting options above to a block of texts, you would need to select the texts. To do this, tap and hold a word, and then drag ⬛ or ⬛ to select the texts you want.

Attaching a file

You can insert an attachment into your message by clicking on **ATTACH** located at the top of the screen. Select whether your attachment is a **DOCUMENT,** a **GALLERY,** or **OTHER (e.g. Samsung notes).** Locate and tap on the file you want to attach.

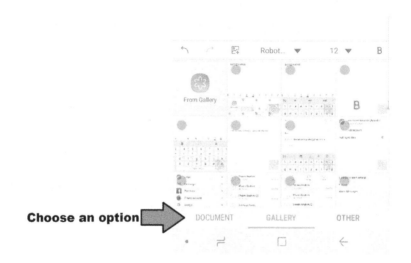

To view saved attachments, go to app screen and tap **Samsung** folder. Tap **My files** and then tap an appropriate content category. Alternatively, visit **Photos/Gallery** app if the attachment is an image.

Managing a Received Email

One of the most important functions of any email app is the ability to receive incoming messages. By default, Email app searches for new messages and alerts you when there is one.

New messages are either stored in Inbox or Junk/Trash/Spam folder and these are the two places to check if you are expecting an email.

To see if there is a new message, swipe down from the top of the screen.

Troubleshooting Tip: If you are not getting notifications from Email app, these are the things to check:

1. Check that you have not blocked notifications from this app. You can know this by following the steps on page 99 and 100.

2. Confirm that you have not disabled **Sync** function. To do this, swipe down from the top of the screen with two fingers. Then swipe left and see if **Sync** appears bold. If it appears bold, then it is enabled. Please note that if *Sync* is disabled you may not get some notifications.

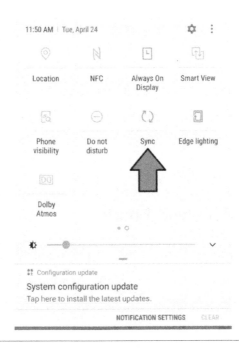

3. If the first two steps above do not work, then make sure your phone is not restricting the Email app's battery usage. Restricting the battery usage for an app might affect the ability of the app to get sync or use data. To know if Email app has a restricted battery usage, go to **Settings** 🔘 >

    Apps > menu icon ⋮ (located at the top of the screen) > **Special access > Optimize battery usage**. Tap the dropdown menu and select **All apps** (see the picture below).

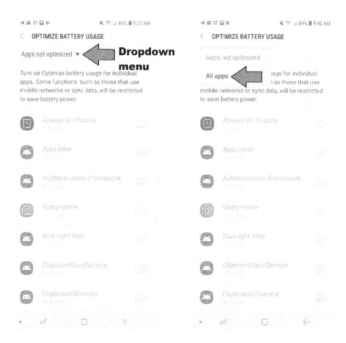

Scroll down and locate the **Email** app and make sure the indicator switch next to it is turned off.

To read a message:

- Tap on the subject of a message to open the message text in the preview pane.

- Those messages that you have not yet read should appear bold.

- A paperclip icon ⬚ means that a message has an attachment.

- The Email app allows you to perform the following actions on a message in your inbox:

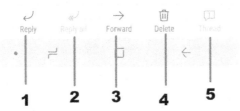

If the icons above are not showing up while viewing an email message, swipe down from the middle of the screen.

1. **Reply:** Tap this button to reply an email message. When you tap this button, a new window appears. This window is similar to what appears when you tap on a new email button but with a slight difference. The reply window contains the recipient's name and the subject. In addition, the original message usually appears at the bottom of your reply for reference.

2. **Reply All:** If the message in your inbox is addressed to several people, you can choose to reply all those people by tapping **Reply All.** You can know whether an email is sent to many people by tapping **Details** tab next to the sender's name/address.

April 24, 2018 11:26 AM

webnet.it   DETAILS

Thank you very much.

3. **Forward:** Use this option to send a copy of an email in your inbox to your friends or associates. When you tap on the **Forward** button, a message window with a subject line preceded by "Fwd:" appears. The original message address (To and From), date, subject, attachment, and text are also usually included. In addition, you will have the option to fill in the email address of the person to whom you are sending the message.

4. **Delete:** Use this option to delete a message from your inbox. Alternatively, tap and hold the email and select **Delete.**

5. **Thread:** This shows the number of conversation you have made.

Hint: When you open the Email app inbox to check a mail, the name of the sender is usually displayed on the top of the message pane. To see the email address of whoever sent the message, tap the mail and then tap the name of the sender and select **View contact**.

In addition, to quickly add an email address to VIP list, simply double tap the name of the sender or email address. To remove it from VIP list, double tap again.

How to Open and Save an Attachment in the Email App

The email with an attachment will have a paper clip icon displayed next to the address of the sender when you check your message inbox.

To open an attachment:

1. Tap the message that has the attachment, as indicated by a

   paper clip icon 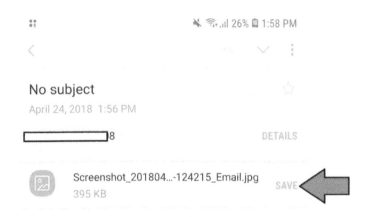 .

2. When the message opens, tap **Save** next to the attachment to

   save it.

If your device is not having an appropriate program to open

the attachment, you may be unable to view the attachment. In

a situation like this, you would need to install the appropriate

program for the type of file. You may ask the person that sent

the message about which program to use to open the

attachment.

3. To view saved attachments, go to app screen and tap

   Samsung folder. Tap **My files** and then tap **Downloads.**

   Alternatively, if the attachment is an image, go to

   Photos/Gallery app.

Managing the Settings Options

Some of the options under Email Settings have already been discussed. But I would still like to briefly mention some few more things.

2. To access the Email app settings, open the Email app and tap menu icon located at the left top corner of the screen.

3. Tap on **Settings** located at the top of the screen.

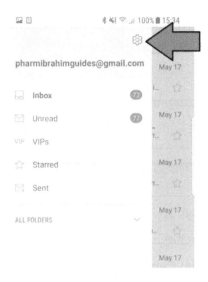

4. Under **General** tab, tap an option. To configure specific settings for an account, tap the account.

5. To delete an account from your device, tap the email account and then tap **REMOVE** next to the account name.

How to Remove the Default Email Signature in the Email App

You can use the Signature tab to command the Email app what signature to include in a message. To do this, open the email app, tap the menu icon ▬ (located at the top of the screen) and then tap

Settings ⚙ . Tap the desired account, tap **Signature**, and then key in a signature of your choice. Tap **DONE** located at the top of the screen. You can use the switch next to Signature to enable or disable this feature.

Note: An email signature is a text that appears by default after the body of your message. You may set your email signature to be your name or brand.

Personal Information

Contacts

This app allows you to create and manage a list of your personal or business contacts. You can save names, mobile phone numbers, home phone numbers, email addresses, and more.

To create a contact:

1. While on the Home screen, swipe up and tap on **Contact** app. If you are using the Contacts app for the first time, follow the onscreen instructions to set it up.

2. Tap on **Add contact** icon located at the lower right corner of the screen.

3. Select where you want to save the contact from the options that appear. To make your selection the default selection, tap **Set As Default.**

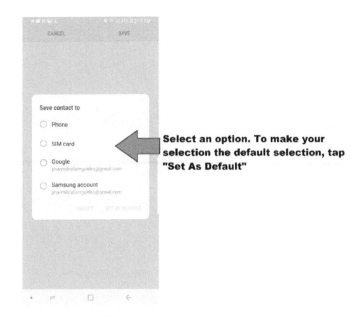

Select an option. To make your selection the default selection, tap "Set As Default"

To change your selection afterward, tap the dropdown arrow next to your selection. See the picture below.

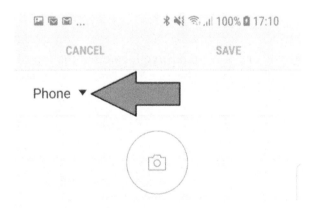

4. Fill in the details by tapping on each item on the screen.
5. To assign a contact to a group, tap **Group.**
6. To access more options, tap on **View more**.

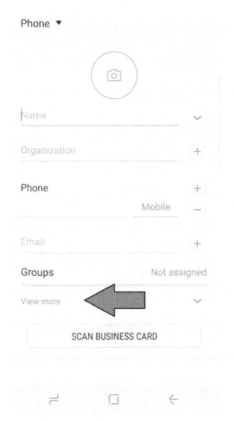

7. When you are done, tap **Save** located at the top of the screen.

Please note that if you choose SIM Card as your storage location in step 3 above, you may not be able to fill more than a name and phone number.

Hint: To search for a contact, open the contact app and tap the **search** bar (located at the top of the screen), and start typing a name. The list filters as you write.

When you receive a message, you can easily save the number if it is not yet saved in your contacts. To do this, tap the messaging app.

Tap a conversation, tap the menu icon located at the top right corner of the screen and tap the phone number in question. Thereafter, tap **Create contact** (located at the bottom of the screen). Follow the on-screen instructions to finish the process.

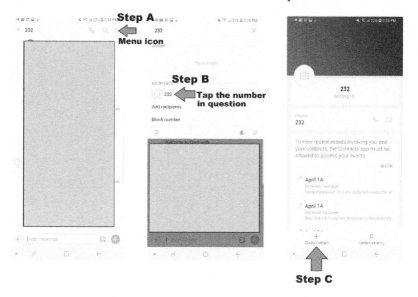

To manage a contact:

1. From the app screen, tap on the **Contact** app.
2. Tap on a contact from the list.
3. Tap the **details** icon (the last icon on the right).

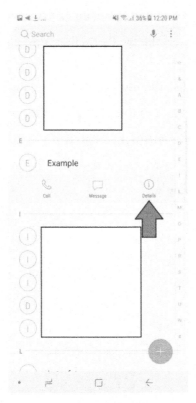

4. To edit a contact, tap **EDIT** located at the top of the screen and then enter the new details. Tap **Save** when you are done.

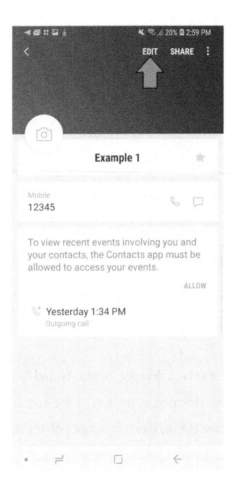

5. To delete a contact, open the contact app, tap and hold the contact you want to delete and then tap on **Delete** located at the top of the screen. You can also use the method to delete many contacts at once. All you have to do is to select all the contacts you want to delete and then tap **Delete**.

6. To share a contact, tap and hold the contact you want to share and then tap **Share.**

To link a contact, tap the contact, tap **Details** and then tap the menu icon ⋮ .

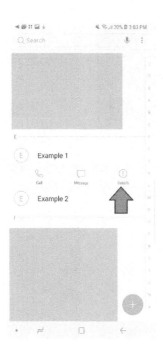 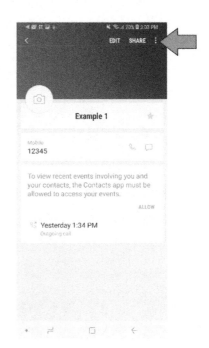

Then tap **Link contacts** or **Merge contacts** and tap the contacts to link with. Tap **Link** (located at the top of the screen). Linking two contacts is important if you have separate entries for the same contact from different social networking services or email accounts. To unlink a contact, tap the contact you want to unlink, tap **Details** and then tap the menu icon ⋮ . Tap **Managed Link contacts** and tap the **Unlink** next to the contact you want to unlink. To link another contact, tap **Link Another Contact**. If you have many contacts linked together, tap **Unlink All** (located at the bottom of the screen) to unlink all of them.

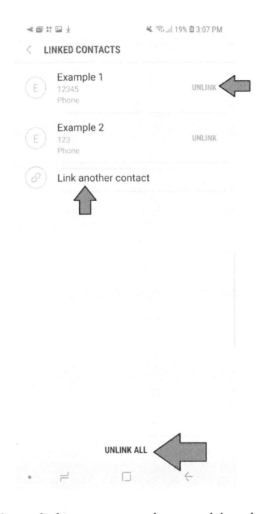

Please note that unlinking a contact does not delete the contact.

Copy contact(s)

If you have some contacts stored on your SIM card, you can copy them to your phone with some simple steps.

1. From the app screen, tap on the **Contact** app.

2. Tap the menu icon ⋮ .

3. Tap **Manage contacts**.

4. Tap **Import/Export contacts**.

5. Tap **Import**.

6. Select where you are copying the contact(s) from.

7. If you want to import all the contacts, tap **ALL** located at the top of the screen. You may also individually select the contacts. To remove a contact you have previously selected, tap the minus icon next to it.

8. Tap **DONE** (located at the top of the screen).

9. Tap **Phone** or where you are sending the contacts to.

10. Tap **Import.** Please note that you can use this method to also copy contacts from SD card and internal storage.

Tip: You can **export** contacts from your phone to other places by following the steps similar to the ones mentioned above. But don't forget that you will select **Export** (and not Import) in step 5.

Contact Group

If you would like to send a message to several people at the same time, I would advise that you create a contact group. You can create a contact group for friends and family members in order to reach them easily.

To create a group:

1. From the app screen, tap on the **Contact**  app.
2. Tap on **Groups.**

3. Tap **Create**.

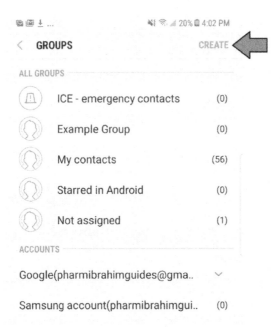

< **GROUPS**   CREATE

ALL GROUPS

(🛕) ICE - emergency contacts   (0)

(👤) Example Group   (0)

(👤) My contacts   (56)

(👤) Starred in Android   (0)

(👤) Not assigned   (1)

ACCOUNTS

Google(pharmibrahimguides@gma..   ⌄

Samsung account(pharmibrahimgui..   (0)

4. Fill in a name for the group, tap **Add member** to add members to the newly created group and tap **Done**.

5. To remove a contact, tap the minus icon next to the contact.

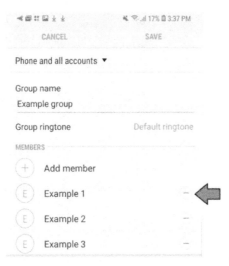

◀ 🖼 ⠿ 🖾 ⏚ ⏚   🔊 🔋 17% 🔋 3:37 PM

     CANCEL   SAVE

Phone and all accounts ▼

Group name
Example group

Group ringtone   Default ringtone

MEMBERS

(+) Add member

(E) Example 1   —

(E) Example 2   —

(E) Example 3   —

6. Tap **Save** (located at the top of the screen).

Please note that you may not be able to add contacts stored on SIM card to contact group.

To add members to a group afterwards:

1. From the app screen, tap on **Contact** app.

2. Tap on **Groups** and tap a group.

3. Tap **Edit.**

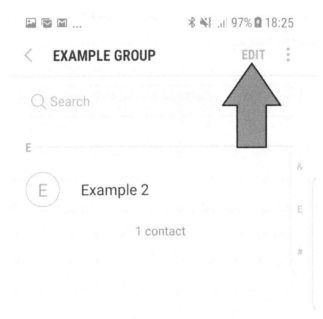

4. Tap **Add Member**. Then tap on a contact to add and tap **Done**.

5. Tap **Save** (located at the top of the screen) to save the changes.

Tip: To remove a contact from a group follow steps 1 to 3 above and then tap the minus icon ⎯ next to the contact you want to remove.

Managing a group contact:

1. From the app screen, tap on the **Contact** app.
2. Tap on **Groups** and tap a group.
3. To send a message to a group, tap **Menu icon** ⋮ and tap **Send message**.

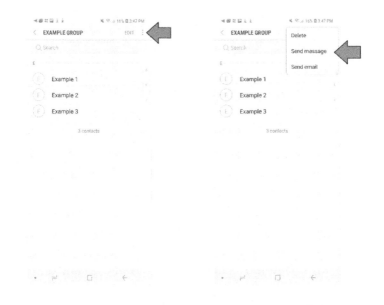

4. To send an email to a group, tap **Menu icon** ⋮ and tap **Send email**. Please note that you may not be able to send email to a group, if you have not added email addresses to the individual contacts in the group.

Deleting a group:

1. From the app screen, tap on the **Contact** app.

2. Tap on **Groups** and tap a group.

3. Tap **Menu icon** ⋮ .

4. Tap **Delete**.

5. Tap **Group only** to delete only the group. Tap **Group and members** to delete both the group and the contact(s) in the group.

Hint: To customize the Contact app, tap on the **Contact** app, tap the **Menu icon** ⋮ and then tap **Settings**.

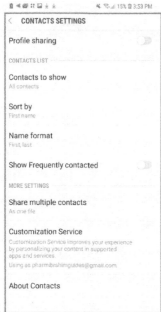

Use these settings options to customize Contact app

Accessibility Features – the Special Features for Easy Usage

Accessibility services are special features for those with physical challenges. In addition, it also provides you the opportunity to control your phone in a special way.

Vision

This option allows you to hear what is happening on the screen as you touch/interact with the phone screen.

To use the vision settings:

1. Swipe down from the top of the screen and select the settings icon ⚙.

2. Scroll down and tap **Accessibility**.

3. Tap **Vision**.

4. Tap the desired option. Interestingly, for complex options, usually, there are explanations beneath them. You can read these explanations to get what each option represents.

Hint: Vision tab contains those settings that help with vision. These settings are particularly good for visually impaired person.

Hearing

This tab allows you to control sound related settings. For example, you can turn off all sounds using this feature.

To use the Hearing settings:

1. Swipe down from the top of the screen and select the settings

    icon .

2. Scroll down and tap **Accessibility.**

3. Tap **Hearing.**

4. Tap the desired option. Interestingly, for complex options, usually, there are explanations beneath them. You can read these explanations to get what each option represents.

Hint: The settings under the hearing tab is particularly good for hearing impaired person. For example, if you are using hearing aid, you can see the settings for your hearing aid under this tab.

In addition, you can turn on the flash notification if you want your phone to flash light when there is a notification.

Flash the camera light or the screen when you receive notifications or when alarms sound.

Camera light

Screen

Dexterity and Interaction

This option allows you to control your device in a special way. For example, you can control your device with your customized switches using the **Universal switches** tab. Although, I would advise you don't tamper with the **Universal switches** unless you know much about it. If you mistakenly switch on **Universal switches** and you wish to turn it off, just press the power button and the volume up button together once.

To use Dexterity and interaction:

1. Swipe down from the top of the screen and select the settings

    icon ⚙ .

2. Scroll down and tap **Accessibility**.

3. Tap **Dexterity and interaction**.

4. Tap the desired option. Interestingly, for complex options, usually, there are explanations beneath them. You can read these explanations to get what each option represents.

Hint: Dexterity and interaction tab contains those settings that help you to control your device with gestures.

More settings

This option allows you to access extra accessibility settings. For example, you can export your accessibility settings and share them with another device using the settings (**Accessibility settings backup**) under this tab.

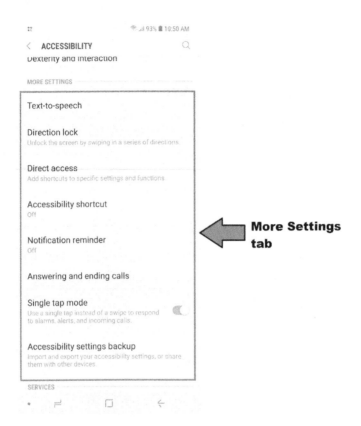

Dexterity and interaction

MORE SETTINGS

Text-to-speech

Direction lock
Unlock the screen by swiping in a series of directions.

Direct access
Add shortcuts to specific settings and functions.

Accessibility shortcut
Off

Notification reminder
Off

Answering and ending calls

Single tap mode
Use a single tap instead of a swipe to respond
to alarms, alerts, and incoming calls.

Accessibility settings backup
Import and export your accessibility settings, or share
them with other devices.

SERVICES

More Settings tab

Services

This tab allows you to access additional accessibility app(s). Any accessibility app downloaded from Google Appstore should appear here.

TOOLS

Easy Mode

Easy mode provides a simpler layout and bigger icons on the Home screen, thereby enhancing visual experience and easier use. Please note that some features may not be available when Easy mode is enabled.

To enable and manage Easy mode:

1. Swipe down from the top of the screen and select settings

   icon ⚙ . Tap **Display** tab.

2. Tap **Easy mode**.
3. Tap **Easy mode** to enable this feature.
4. If available, use the switch next to each app to add or remove.
5. Tap **Apply** located at the top of the screen to save your settings. Then tap the Home key to return to the Home screen.
6. When Easy mode is enabled, you can add a shortcut to your favorite contacts. To add a shortcut to a contact; from the Home screen, swipe the screen to the right. Then tap the plus icon and follow the prompts.

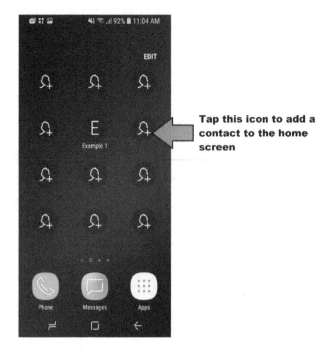

Tap this icon to add a
contact to the home
screen

To disable Easy mode:

1. Swipe down from the top of the screen and select settings

   icon ⚙. Tap **Display** tab.

2. Scroll down and tap **Easy mode**.

3. Tap **Standard mode** to exit Easy mode.

4. Tap **Apply** to effect the changes.

Do Not Disturb

Do not disturb gives you the opportunity to prevent unnecessary disturbances from your phone. To quickly access this feature and customize it, swipe down from the top of the screen using two fingers and then tap and hold **Do Not disturb** for two seconds. Please note that you may need to swipe to the right to access more quick settings options before you can see **Do Not disturb** icon.

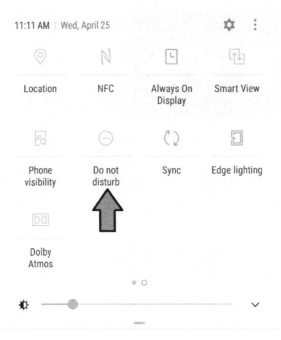

Then select an option.

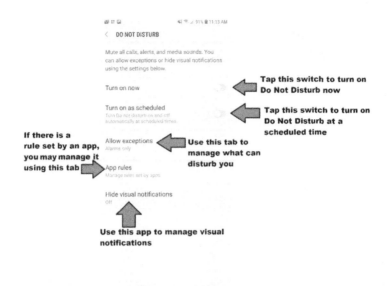

If you choose to schedule Do Not Disturb, then use **Days, Start time** and **End time** to customize your experience. Thereafter, tap the back button to save the changes.

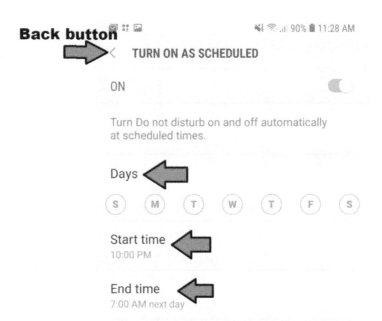

Back button

TURN ON AS SCHEDULED

ON

Turn Do not disturb on and off automatically at scheduled times.

Days

S M T W T F S

Start time
10:00 PM

End time
7:00 AM next day

Please note that when Do Not Disturb is running, you may not get voice feedback from Bixby instead you will only get text feedback.
Hint: There is a feature on your phone called **Blue Light Filter,** Samsung claims this feature can help you sleep better. If you are having difficulty sleeping while using your phone, you may try using this feature. To use this feature:

Swipe down from the top of the screen and tap **Settings** ⚙ > **Display > Blue Light Filter > Turn on now**.

To schedule Blue Light Filter, tap the switch next to **Turn on as scheduled** and the choose an option.

Creating Schedules and More with the Calendar App

Your phone provides you with **Calendar** app to help you organize your schedules and tasks more conveniently and effectively. You can create schedules and add events.

> ➤ **To create an event:**

1. From the Home screen, swipe up and tap on **Calendar** .

2. Tap the plus icon at the lower right side of the screen and enter the details.

3. To set the start and the end date of the event, tap **Start/End.**

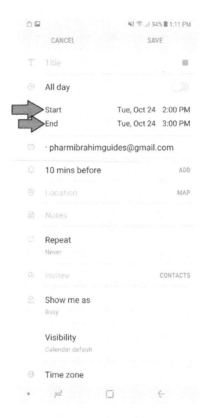

CANCEL   SAVE

T   Title   ▦

⊙   All day   ⚪⟩

▶ Start   Tue, Oct 24   2:00 PM
▶ End   Tue, Oct 24   3:00 PM

▭   · pharmibrahimguides@gmail.com

🔔   10 mins before   ADD

◎   Location   MAP

▤   · Notes

▭   Repeat
    Never

ጸ   Invitee   CONTACTS

🔒   Show me as
    Busy

    Visibility
    Calendar default

⊕   Time zone

•   ⇄   ▢   ←

4. When you are done, tap **Save** (located at the top of the screen).

Hint: Your phone will give you a notification when the time for an event arrives.

> ➢ **To view an event/schedule:**

1. From the Home screen, swipe up and tap on **Calendar** 📅.

2. To change the calendar view, tap **View** (located at the top of the screen).

3. Tap the desired view.

4. Then tap on an event to view.

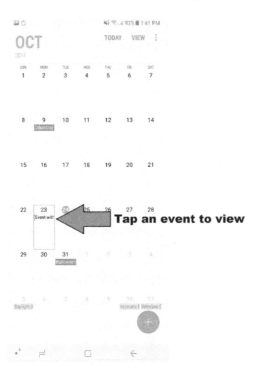

Tap an event to view

➢ **To edit, share or delete an event:**

1. From the Home screen, swipe up and tap on **Calendar** .

2. To change the calendar view, tap **View** (located at the top of the screen). Tap the desired view.

3. Then tap on an event to view.

4. To delete an event, tap and hold the event and select **Delete**.

5. To share an event, tap and hold the event and select **Share**.

6. To edit an event, tap and hold the event and select **Edit**.

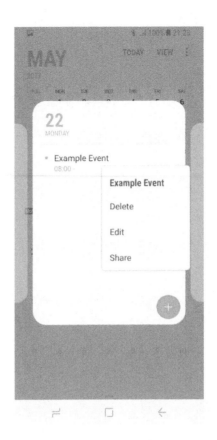

➢ **To change your calendar view**

1. From the Home screen, swipe up and tap on **Calendar.**

2. To change the calendar view, tap **View** (located at the top of the screen). Tap the desired view.

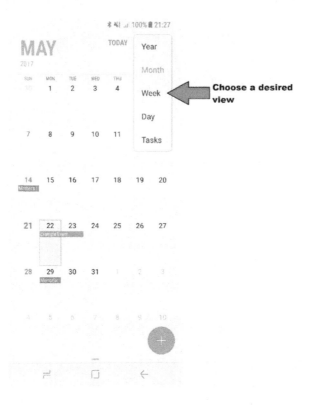

Hint: To customize the calendar app, from the Home screen, swipe

up and tap **Calendar** . Tap the menu icon ⋮ at the top of the

screen. Tap **settings** and choose an option.

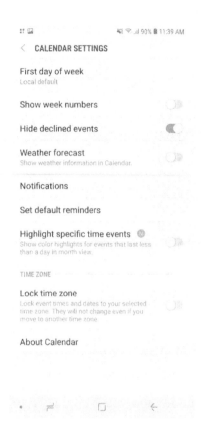

Using the Camera

Samsung Galaxy S9/S9 Plus comes with rear-facing camera(s), a front-facing camera and an LED flash. With these cameras, you can capture an image or record a video.

Note: The memory capacity of the images taken may differ depending on the settings, shooting scenes and shooting conditions.

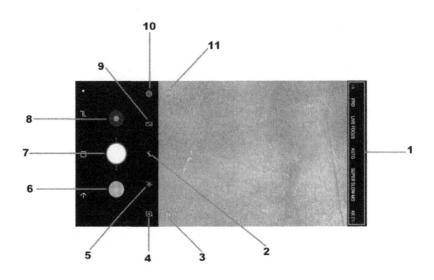

Number	Function
1.	Shooting mode: Camera app has many shooting modes and you would need to choose the shooting mode based on what you are doing. For example, if you are taking a picture of a recipe (food), you can consider using food mode. In addition, if you are taking a picture of waterfall, you can consider using panorama mode. Interestingly, your phone can also determine the ideal shooting mode for you whenever you access the camera. If you don't know which mode to choose, then make sure **Auto** is selected. To select another shooting mode, swipe left or right, or tap the name of the shooting mode.
2.	Flash light button

3.	Zoom button
4.	Front-facing/rear-facing camera switch
5.	Filters button
6.	Preview thumbnail tab
7.	Camera button
8.	Video button
9.	Expand View/Full View
10.	Camera settings
11.	Bixby Vision button. Tap this icon to get more information about the picture you are viewing. To learn more about Bixby vision, please go to page 198.

> ➤ **To Capture a photo**

1. While the phone is locked, double-press the Power Key (at the side of the phone) to launch the camera app. Please note that you may need to enable this feature. To do this, see page 306. Alternatively, from the app screen, tap **Camera.**

2. Aim the lens at the subject and make any necessary adjustments. To focus any part of the screen, tap that part of the screen.

3. To adjust the picture size, tap settings ⚙ and then tap the **Picture size**. Please note that the picture size you pick may affect the memory size of your captured image.

4 Tap **front-facing/rear-facing icon** to switch between the front-facing and rear-facing cameras.

5. To zoom in, place two fingers on the screen and spread them apart. Do the reverse to zoom out.

6. Tap on **camera button** when you are done adjusting the settings.

Note: You can choose to enable or disable **Review pictures**. To disable **Review pictures,** tap the settings icon ⚙ while on the camera app, scroll down and tap the switch next to **Review pictures**. When the image review is enabled, you will see a preview of each photo immediately after you take a picture. This allows you to immediately delete the picture if you are not satisfied with it.

Tip: To change the picture storage location to SD card, while on the camera app screen, tap the settings icon ⚙ and then scroll down and tap **Storage Location.** Then select **SD card** from the option that appears.

To open the Camera by quickly pressing the Power key twice:

1. Swipe down from the top of the screen and select the settings icon

.

2. Tap **Advanced features.**

3. Tap the switch next to **Quick launch camera** to activate it.

To customize camera settings:

1. When the phone is locked, double-press the Power Key (at the side of the phone) to launch the camera app. Alternatively, from the Home screen, tap **Camera.**

2. Tap the settings icon 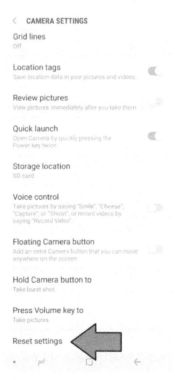 .

3. Adjust the various settings as you like.

Hint: Camera settings consist of a lot of features, and you may not need to touch some of these features. In fact, the default settings are enough for many users.

If someone adjusts the camera settings the way you don't like, and you wish to restore the camera settings to factory settings, follow these steps. Tap the settings icon while on the camera app screen, scroll down and tap **Reset settings.** Tap **Reset** when prompted.

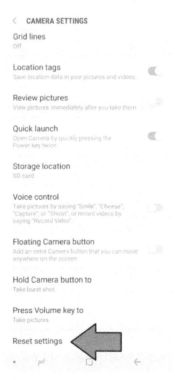

Recording a video

1. When the phone is locked, double-press the Power Key (at the side of the phone) to launch the camera app. Please note that you may need to enable this feature. To do this, see page 306. Alternatively, from the Home screen, tap **Camera.**

2 Tap on the video button ▣ to start recording.

3. To zoom in while recording, place two fingers on the screen and spread them apart. To zoom out, move the two fingers closer together.

4. When done with the recording, tap the **video button** ◉ again.

6. To view your recorded videos, go to **Gallery/Photos** app.

Editing Your Photos

You can use your phone to edit photos.

1. Swipe up the screen while on the Home screen and tap on **Gallery/Photos**.

2. Tap on the photo you want to edit.

3. Tap the **Edit icon** 🎨 and then pick any editing tool(s).

Getting Productive with Camera

Many people use the camera of their phone just to take pictures, but don't know that they can actually be more productive using the camera on their phones.

Interestingly, Samsung Galaxy S9/S9 Plus features a powerful camera that transforms the way you use phone camera. In this part of the guide, we will be exploring ways you can be more productive with your phone's camera.

Ways to be more productive with your phone camera are mentioned below:

- Use your phone camera as a scanner for your documents

You probably have many documents that are very important to you. Why don't you look for time to take the pictures of all these documents and save them to your phone or have them stored in the cloud. There are times that you would want to check something inside a document, but you are not at home, saving your document on your phone should help you in time like this. In addition, saving documents on your phone will save you time and stress because you have access to them on the go.

- Take picture of natural environment like waterfall and natural vegetation

According to reports, looking at the pictures of natural environment like waterfall and natural vegetation gives people pleasure and serve as a coolness to ones eyes. In addition, it helps you appreciate the beautiful work of Almighty God.

- Declutter your life

Do you know that you can use the camera of your phone to declutter your life? You probably have many hand-written documents, business cards, to-do list etc. lying all over the places in your home. You can take the picture of these notes so that you can remove them from your house and give them to appropriate waste recycling company. This will create more space in your house and give you visual ventilation.

I would advise you properly label the pictures of your hand-written documents, business cards, to-do list etc. so as to help you easily find them in the future. In addition, you can consider saving the pictures of your hand-written documents, business cards, to-do list etc. on *Evernote*. I suggest Evernote because it gives you opportunity to search text inside images.

- Use your camera as a barcode and QR (quick response) code scanner

Barcode and QR code are machine readable codes that are used to store information. Barcode is a linear or one dimensional in nature. It basically looks like a cluster of parallel lines. On the other hand, QR code is two dimensional in nature. An example of a QR code is shown below. Interestingly, Samsung Galaxy S9/S9 Plus is capable of reading QR codes and barcodes using **Bixby vision** or barcode scanner apps. Many of us still take the long path of entering texts or links when we can get the same result by scanning barcode or QR code.

Example of a QR code

To use Bixby vision to scan a QR code:

1. Launch the phone camera and tap Bixby vision icon.

Bixby vision icon

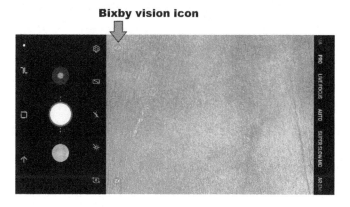

2. Then scroll left and tap **QR code**.

Scroll left and tap QR code

3. Aim your lens at the code and wait for response.

I noticed that Bixby vision can occasionally perform poorly when scanning barcodes and therefore I would advise you install third party barcode scanner app. You can install a barcode scanner from Google Appstore, simply search for *barcode scanner* or *QR and barcode scanner*.

- Take the pictures of notes in a meetings and lecture instead of writing it

Taking the picture of notes after a meeting and lecture allows you to listen during the meeting or lecture instead of writing notes.

- Use your camera to take pictures of valuable information in your life

If you have any valuable piece of information that you can't afford to lose, use your camera to take its picture. That would serve as a backup in case of lost.

Connectivity

Computer Connections

Your phone can be connected to a computer with a USB cable. This would enable you to transfer items such as audio, document and image files to your phone from your computer.

Warning: Do not disconnect the USB cable from a computer while the device is transferring or accessing data. This may result in data loss or damage to your phone.

Transferring content via USB

1. Connect your device to a computer with an appropriate USB cable (like the one that came with your phone).

2. When prompted to allow an access to phone data, tap **Allow.** If you don't choose Allow, your computer may not connect to your phone.

3. Slide down from the top of the screen, tap the USB option (**USB for file transfer**) and tap it again.

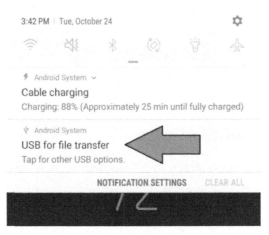

4. Tap **Transfer Files** (if not selected).

5. Your Samsung Galaxy S9/S9 Plus should appear in the same location where an external USB drives usually appear. For

Windows users, this is typically under "This PC/Computer" menu.

6. Open your device drive to see the different folders present. Note that you may not be able to access the folders if your phone is locked.

7. To transfer files from your computer to your phone. Locate the file you want to transfer on your computer. Then click, drag and drop the file into the corresponding folder on your Phone. For example, document files should be dragged to My Documents folder. Alternatively, if you are using PC, right-click on the file you want to send, select **Send to** and then choose your phone from the options that appear.

8. Disconnect your phone just as you would disconnect an external memory drive. If you are using Windows 10, you may just remove the USB from the phone when you are done with the transfer. You may not need to click any disconnect icon before you remove your phone if you are using Windows 10.

Note: After the transfer, your transferred files should appear under the corresponding content library on your device. To view any of the transferred files:

From the Home screen, swipe up and tap **Samsung folder** >
My Files. Then tap an appropriate category to view the transferred files or folders.

Note that your phone will only recognize the file you transferred if the file is a supported file type.

If you do factory reset to your phone, you may need to re-transfer the files again (unless you have them stored on a cloud storage like Dropbox).

Wi-Fi

Using your phone, you can connect to the internet or other network devices anywhere an access point or wireless hotspot is available.

To activate the Wi-Fi feature and connect to a network:

1. Swipe down from the top of the screen.

2. Tap and hold the **Wi-Fi** 🛜 icon.

3. Tap the switch next to Wi-Fi to turn it on.

4. Your device then automatically scans for available networks and displays them.

5. Select a network and enter a password for the network (if necessary). You may also manually add a network. To manually add a network, scroll down (if necessary) and tap **Add network**. Then follow the on-screen instructions.

6. To turn Wi-Fi off, swipe down from the top of the screen and tap **Wi-Fi** 🛜 .

Notes:

- The Wi-Fi feature running in the background will consume battery. To save battery, put it off whenever you are not using it.

- The Wi-Fi may not connect a network if the network signal is not good.

- When Wi-Fi is connected, active, and communicating with a wireless Access Point, Wi-Fi active icon is displayed on the Status bar.

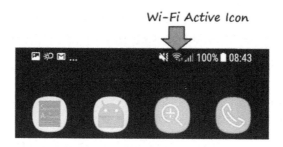

Using Your Phone as a Hotspot

If your network provider supports it, you can use this feature to share your mobile network with friends.

1. Swipe down from the top of the screen and select the settings icon ⚙. Tap **Connections** tab.

2. Tap **Mobile Hotspot and Tethering**.

3. Tap **Mobile hotspot**. If prompted to enable or disable Wi-Fi sharing, you can choose to disable Wi-Fi sharing. Wi-Fi

sharing allows you to share your Wi-Fi connections with other devices, while mobile hotspot shares your mobile data with other devices. Please before you share a Wi-Fi connection with other devices, please ensures that you are not breaking any terms and conditions.

4. Next to Mobile Hotspot, tap **On**. Please note that Wi-Fi would need to be turned off for you to turn on mobile hotspot.

5. To set the password and enable password protection, tap the menu icon ⋮ (located at the top of the screen) and tap **Configure Mobile Hotspot.** Enter a name for the network (this is the name that other devices searching for the network will see). Scroll down and tap **Password**. Then enter a password for the network and tap **Save**.

6. After enabling the mobile hotspot, your friends should be able to connect to it just like they connect to wireless networks.

Hints:

You can choose who connect to your mobile hotspot by creating the Allowed Device list. To do this:

1. Follow steps 1 to 4 above.

2. Tap the menu icon ⋮ > **Allowed devices**, and then tap **Add** to enter the device name and MAC address. The MAC address of many smart gadgets is found under **Wi-Fi settings** or **Wi-Fi Advanced settings.**

4. Tap **Add** to add the device.

5. Tap the status switch next to **Allowed devices only** to make sure only the allowed devices can connect to your mobile hotspot.

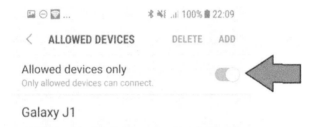

6. To delete an allowed device, tap and hold the device and select **DELETE.**

In addition, you can automatically turn off Mobile hotspot if there are no connected devices. To do this, follow the step 1 above. Then tap the menu icon ⋮ > **Timeout settings**, and then select a time.

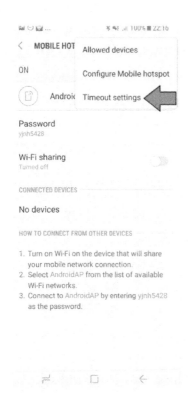

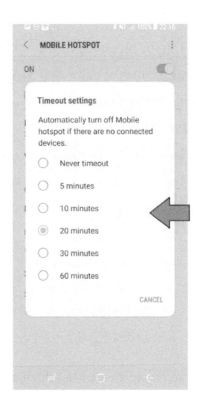

Access More by Using Bluetooth

Bluetooth option allows you to connect to another Bluetooth device within range.

Note: If there are obstacles, the operating distance of the Bluetooth may be reduced. The Bluetooth communication range is usually approximately 30 feet.

To use Bluetooth feature:

1. Swipe down from the top of the screen.

2. Tap and hold the **Bluetooth** icon .

3. Then next to **Bluetooth**, select **on.**

4. Then Bluetooth automatically scans for nearby Bluetooth devices and displays them. Please make sure the Bluetooth of the device you are connecting with is turned on and discoverable.

5. Tap a device to connect with and follow the prompts to finish the connection. You may need to enter a pairing code.

6. When Bluetooth is enabled, the **Bluetooth icon** would appear next to the **Wi-Fi icon** on the Status bar. Pairing between two Bluetooth devices should be a one-time process. Once two devices are paired, the devices may continue to recognize this association and you may not need to re-enter a passcode.

7. To turn Bluetooth off, swipe down from the top of the screen, tap **Bluetooth** . The Bluetooth would appear gray when you turn it off (see the picture below).

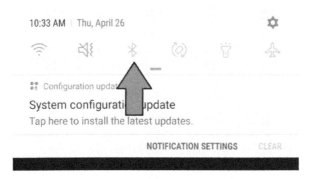

Unpairing a Paired Device

1. Swipe down from the top of the screen.

2. Tap and hold the **Bluetooth** icon.

3. Then next to **Bluetooth**, select **on** (if not already turned on).

4. Tap the settings icon ⚙ next to the paired device, and then tap **Unpair** to delete the paired device.

Tip: Once you have paired your device to another device, you can rename the paired device to make it easier to recognize. To do this,

follow the steps 1 to 3 above and tap the settings icon ⚙ next to the previously paired device. Then tap **Rename**. Enter a new name, and tap **Rename**.

Location Services

Enabling location service allows apps to serve you content related services.

To activate location services:

1. Swipe down from the top of the screen and select the settings icon ⚙ . Tap **Connection.**

2. Tap **Location.**

3. Next to the switch under **Location**, select **on.**

4. To put it off, tap the switch again.

Tip: If you want your phone to use the combination of Wi-Fi, GPS, and mobile networks to estimate your location, tap **Location Method** and then tap **High accuracy.**

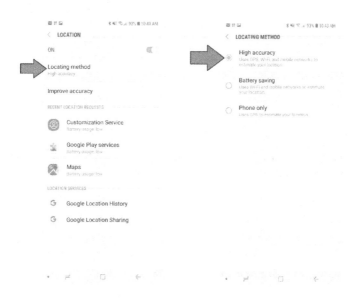

Find My Mobile Feature

You can use this feature to locate your phone if lost.

Note: You must sign up for a Samsung account and enable location service (as explained above) to use **Find My Mobile**.

To add Samsung account (if you have not done so before):

1. Swipe down from the top of the screen and select the settings

   icon .

2. Tap **Cloud and accounts**.

3. Tap **Account**.

4. Tap **Add account**.

5. Tap **Samsung Account**. Then enter your Samsung account information.

6. Or tap **Create Account** and follow the prompts. Please note that if you have already added Samsung account, you can skip these steps.

To activate Find My Mobile Feature:

1. Swipe down from the top of the screen and select the settings icon ⚙ .

2. Tap **Lock screen and security**.

3. Scroll down and tap **Find My Mobile**.

4. If required, enter your Samsung account's password and then tap **Sign In.** If you don't have a Samsung account, create one.

5. Make sure that the status switches beside **Remote Controls, Google Location Service** and **Send Last Location** are turned on.

To find your lost phone:

1. Open a web browser **findmymobile.samsung.com**

2. Tap **Sign In.**

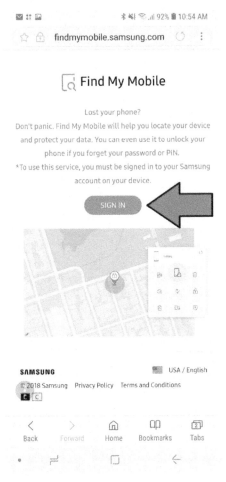

3. Enter the email address associated with your Samsung account into the email field and then enter your password. Click **Sign In.**

4. If you have more than one Samsung phone, you may need to select your Samsung Galaxy S9/S9 Plus (if it is not currently displayed). To do this, tap the menu icon ≡ next to the current device name and select your device name.

5. Tap the dropdown icon to access the map.

Device location found

Galaxy S9+

Checking status...

Locating your p...

LAST LOCATION U...

Apr 26th, 10:56 A...

Dropdown icon

Ring   Lock   Erase data

Back up   Retrieve calls/messages   Unlock

Extend battery life   Set guardian

Back   Forward   Home   Bookmarks   Tabs

6. To close the map, tap the V-shaped icon.

V-shaped icon

The current location of your phone will be displayed on a map.
You can use the options on this website to **ring your device, lock your device, back up your device, extend battery life, set guardian and wipe/erase your device**.

Tip: You can use **Find My Device** to unlock your device when you forget your log in information. To do this, follow the steps 1-4 above and tap **Unlock** and enter your Samsung account password.

Note: Please note that your phone may need to be connected to a wireless or mobile network to be able to use the **Find My Mobile** feature to manage your phone. However, you may still be able to know the last known location of your phone.

Using the NFC (Near Field Communication)

This is a technology like Bluetooth and Wi-Fi. It utilizes electromagnetic radio frequency. Devices using NFC may be passive or active. A passive device is not powered by battery but contains information that other devices can read but does not read any information itself. An example of a passive NFC is NFC tag. On the other hand, an active NFC device can read information and send it. An example of an active NFC device is your Samsung Galaxy S9/S9 Plus.

You can use NFC feature to send files from your phone to other NFC supported devices.

To turn on and use NFC:

1. Swipe down from the top of the screen using two fingers then

   tap and hold the **NFC** icon for two seconds. Please note that you may need to swipe to the right to access more quick settings options before you can see the **NFC** icon.

2. Under **NFC and payment,** tap the switch to turn it on. Also make sure the status switch next to **Android Beam** is turned on.

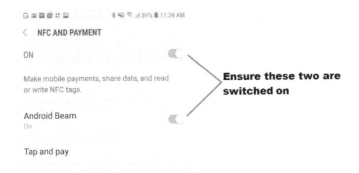

ON

Make mobile payments, share data, and read or write NFC tags.

Ensure these two are switched on

Android Beam
On

Tap and pay

3. To use NFC to send a file to another device, ensure both devices involved have their NFC turned on. Then open the file you wish to send and tap **Share**. Tap **Android Beam**. Hold your mobile phone and the receiving device back to back. Then tap the screen to send the file.

It may not be very effective in sending large files because it may be slow.

Using NFC to make payment

In recent times, NFC is finding more usage in payment system.

Making payments with the NFC feature:

1. Follow steps 1 and 2 above (under **To turn on and use NFC**).

2. Touch the back of your device to the NFC card reader.

Usually, after you have enabled NFC payments on your phone, you should be able to make payments for items by tapping your phone against a participating store's NFC reader.

For best results, place the center part of the phone against the NFC reader.

You can select the default payment application you want to use for making purchases on your device if you have more than one payment method installed. To do this, when on the **NFC and payment** screen, tap **Tap and pay** and then tap **PAYMENT** (located at the top of the screen). Then select a default payment app.

Settings

Settings menu give you the opportunity to customize your device as you like.

To access the settings menu

1. Swipe down from the top of the screen and select the settings icon ⚙ .

2. Alternatively, swipe up from the Home screen and then tap **Settings**.

3. Tap a setting category.

Search for Settings

It is advisable to use the searching feature when you are not sure exactly where to find a certain setting.

1. Swipe down from the top of the screen and select the settings icon ⚙ .

2. Tap Search bar.

3. Enter a word or words in the Search field. The list filters as you write.

4. Tap an option (make sure you select the best match).

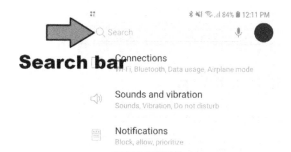

Search bar

Connections
Wi-Fi, Bluetooth, Data usage, Airplane mode

Sounds and vibration
Sounds, Vibration, Do not disturb

Notifications
Block, allow, prioritize

Hint: There is a tip to getting what you want from your device. From time to time, you would want to customize your phone in a special way. All you need to do in a period like this is to open the settings as described above. Then tap the search bar and enter a search word or phrase corresponding to what you want to do.

What You Must Know About Samsung Galaxy S9/S9 Plus

How to Find Your Phone When lost

As a human being, it is not impossible that you may misplace your phone. If someone else (a thief) has not taken custody of it, there are steps to follow to find it. These steps have been discussed at length in the preceding chapter (see page 323-330); please refer to it for details.

How to Reduce Your Mobile Data Usage on Samsung Galaxy S9/S9 Plus

If you realize that you are using more MB/Data than normal, there are steps to follow to reduce your data consumption.

1. The first thing is to make sure that you update apps on Wi-Fi only. To do this:
   a. Swipe up from the Home screen and tap **Play Store**.
   b. Tap the menu icon.

Menu icon

c. Tap **Settings**.

d. Tap **Auto-update apps** and select **Auto-update apps over Wi-Fi only.**

2. Consider using a data friendly browser: Browser like **Opera Mini** gives you the opportunity to save data through their **data saving** feature. You can also control the picture quality of webpages when you are using Opera Mini browser and thereby saving data. To download Opera Mini, please visit Google Play store.

3. Enable Data saver: To do this, from a Home screen, tap the settings icon ⚙ . Tap **Connections**. Tap **Data usage** and then tap **Data saver**. Tap the status switch next to **Data saver**.

To control the number of apps that have unrestricted access to your data, tap **Allow app while Data saver on.**

4. Use the **Datally** app. This app allows you to save and control the use of your data. To download Datally, please visit Google Play store.

Solution to Non-Responding Apps

Sometimes an app may start misbehaving and may even refuse to close. The first thing you can do in a situation like this is to tap on the recent button [icon]. This gives you an access to all opened/running apps on your phone. Locate this app, and tap **X** icon to close it. Try launching the app again.

If it is still misbehaving after closing it or it refuses to close, then you may try these steps:

1. Swipe down from the top of the screen and select the settings icon [icon].
2. Tap **Apps**.
3. Then tap on the misbehaving application from the list of applications.
4. Select **FORCE STOP**. This will stop the app from carrying out any process on your phone. To enable the app again, just launch the app.

Note: Please restart your device if stopping an app causes your device to stop working correctly. *In addition, force stopping an app may cause error(s).*

How to Conserve Samsung Galaxy S9/S9 Plus's Battery Life

You may notice that you have to charge Samsung Galaxy S9/S9 Plus twice in 24 hours to keep it on. There are steps to follow to ensure that your phone serves you throughout the day with just a single charge.

1. **Reduce the screen brightness and turn off the automatic brightness:** I have realized over time that screen brightness consumes a lot of energy. There is usually a substantial difference between using a phone with a maximum brightness and using it with a moderate brightness. As a rule, don't use your phone with a maximum brightness unless you can't see what is on the screen clearly. For example, if you are outdoor. Make sure you reduce it immediately when it is no more needed.

   To reduce the screen brightness, swipe down from the top of the screen using two fingers. Then use the small circle on the slider to adjust the brightness.

To manage Auto brightness, tap the **dropdown arrow** next to the brightness slider and then tap the switch next to **Auto brightness**.

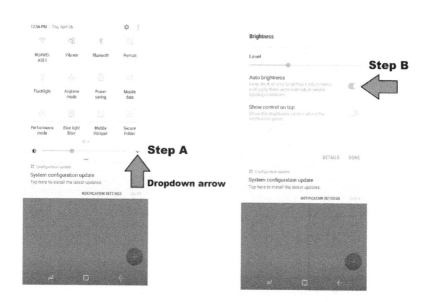

2. **Shorten the Screen timeout:** if you really want to save your battery life, you must try to shorten the screen timeout.

Reducing how long your phone would stay lit up after you finish interacting with it will help you to save your battery. To manage screen timeout setting:

a. Swipe down from the top of the screen and select the settings icon 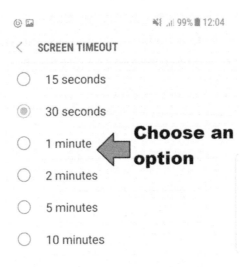 .

b. Tap **Display**.

c. Scroll down and tap on **Screen Timeout**. Then choose an option.

3. **Turn off Wi-Fi and Bluetooth:** when you are not using Wi-Fi or Bluetooth, please always remember to put them off. These features really consume energy and they are better off when not in use.

4. **Reduce number of notifications:** there are two benefits of doing this. The first is that there will be less distractions and

the second benefit is that notification consumes energy. Limit yourself to those notifications that are important to your life. To manage notification setting for an app:

a. Swipe down from the top of the screen and select the

settings icon .

b. Tap **Apps**.

c. Tap an app.

d. Tap on **Notifications** to configure the notifications setting for the chosen app. To disable the notification for an app, tap the indicator switch next to **On.**

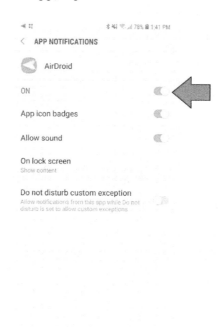

5. **Close all unnecessary apps:** the truth is that any app you are accessing is consuming out of the limited battery energy. It is important to close any app you are not using from time to time. To access all apps currently running on your phone, tap on the recent button and then tap **X** icon next to the application you want to close. Alternatively, swipe left or right to close an app.

6. **Use a correct charger:** using a wrong charger can endanger the health of your phone/battery, and it is better to avoid such practice.

7. **Consider switching off your phone:** if you are not going to use your phone for an extended period, you may consider switching off your phone.

What to Do if You Forget You Device Lock Screen Password/Pin

1. Open a web browser **findmymobile.samsung.com**

2. Tap **Sign In.**

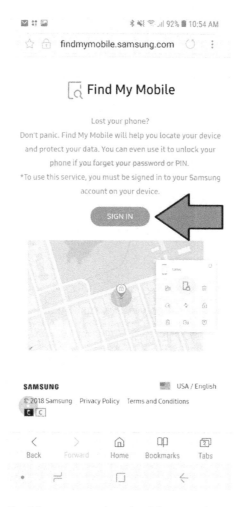

3. Enter the email address associated with your Samsung account into the email field and then enter your password. Click **Sign In.**

4. If you have more than one Samsung phone, you may need to select your Samsung Galaxy S9/S9 Plus (if it is not currently displayed). To do this, tap the menu icon ☰ next to the current device name and select your device name.

5. Tap **Unlock** and enter your Samsung account password.

Note: Your phone may need to be connected to a wireless or mobile network to be able to use the **Find My Mobile** feature to unlock your phone.

In addition, please note that if you have disabled **Remote Controls**, you would need to activate it before you can use the method above. To do this:

1. Swipe down from the top of the screen and select the settings icon ⚙.

2. Tap **Lock screen and security**.

3. Tap **Find My Mobile**.

4. Enter your Samsung account information and then tap **Sign In.** If you don't have a Samsung account, then create one.

5. Make sure that the status switches beside **Remote Controls**, **Google Location Service** and **Send Last Location** are turned on.

How to Take Screenshot on Your Device

Another task you can perform on your device is taking a screenshot. To take a screenshot with your device, please follow the instructions below:

Method 1

Press and hold the volume down key and the power key simultaneously until you hear a small sound/vibration. You can view captured images in Gallery.

Method 2

You can also capture screenshots by swiping your hand to the left or right across the screen. To be able to use this method, you have to enable it. To do this:

1. Swipe down from the top of the screen and select the settings icon

⚙ .

2. Scroll down and tap **Advanced features**.

3. Tap **Palm swipe to capture** and then tap the status switch to activate it.

To capture a screenshot when this feature is enabled, just swipe the edge of your hand across more than half of the screen.

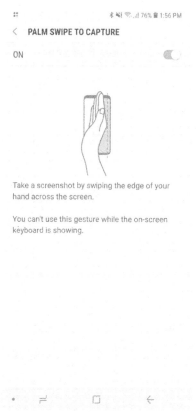

Take a screenshot by swiping the edge of your hand across the screen.

You can't use this gesture while the on-screen keyboard is showing.

The Smart Capture

You can capture a screen and the scrollable area. In addition, you can immediately crop and share the captured screen. This feature is usually enabled by default, but if you want to check whether it is enabled or not, please follow the instructions below:

1. Swipe down from the top of the screen and select the settings icon

 .

2. Scroll down and tap **Advanced features**.

3. Tap **Smart capture**, and then tap the status switch to activate it.

Thereafter, press and hold the volume down key and the power key simultaneously to take a screenshot. Then tap on any of these options below:

Bixby Vision: Tap this icon to get more information about the screenshot you have captured. To learn more about Bixby Vision, see page 198.

Scroll Capture: Use this to capture the hidden parts of the screen. When you tap this icon, the screen will automatically scroll down, and more content would be captured. To capture more screen, tap this icon again.

Draw: Use this option to annotate the screenshot.

Crop: Use this to crop a portion from the screenshot.

Share: Use this to share the screenshot.

Extras

What You Must Know Before Selling or Giving Away Your Samsung Galaxy S9/S9 Plus

A time would probably come when you may need to give away or sell your Samsung Galaxy S9/S9 Plus. There are few things you must know before this time comes.

Some time ago, BBC reported that Avast (an antivirus giant) was able to use publicly available forensic security tools to extracts naked selfies from second-hand phones bought on eBay. Other extracted data were emails, text messages and Google searches. It is usual for many users to perform factory resets before selling their phones. The truth is that with the advent of sophisticated software, factory reset is no more enough. In fact, you have to go a step further.

So, what can you do to save your privacy? The simple answer is to go a step further by always encrypting your files. You should encrypt all your data before performing factory reset when you are considering selling or giving away your Phone.

However, you must know that encrypting your device before doing the factory reset may not give 100% protection to your privacy. Who knows if programmers will develop a software that will be a step ahead of that in the nearest future? The best way to completely protect your privacy is to destroy your phone when you don't need it again. But as you know, this is not feasible all the time and may not be advisable.

Finally, encrypting your phone before performing factory reset is an efficient way of protecting your privacy. At least it makes it much more difficult for people to retrieve your files.

Interestingly, Samsung Galaxy S9/S9 Plus automatically encrypts data stored on it. However, you would need to encrypt data stored on memory card yourself. To do that:

- From the Home screen, swipe up from the bottom of the screen and tap **Settings**.

- Tap **Lock screen and security > Encrypt SD card**.

- Read the onscreen information and if you are satisfied with it, tap **Encrypt SD card**.

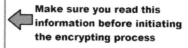
< **ENCRYPT SD CARD**

You can encrypt SD cards. Encrypted SD cards can only be read on the device used to encrypt them. Tap ENCRYPT SD CARD to start the encryption process.

Encryption could take an hour or more. Before you start, make sure that the battery is charged and keep the device plugged in until encryption is complete. During the encryption process, the SD card cannot be used. If your device is reset to factory default settings, it will be unable to read encrypted SD cards.

Make sure you read this information before initiating the encrypting process

ENCRYPT SD CARD

When you encrypt your memory card, you may need a numeric PIN or password to decrypt your SD card when you first access it after switching on your device.

Getting an antivirus for your phone -- is it necessary?

Many people may not really take the issue of antivirus seriously because they think that virus software target PC much more than phones. The truth is that things are changing every now and then. The best thing you can do is to always keep a guard.

Interestingly, there is a device protection on Samsung Galaxy S9/S9 Plus, to access this protection:

- From the Home screen, swipe up from the bottom of the screen and tap **Settings**.

- Tap **Device Maintenance**

- Tap **Device security** (located at the lower right part of the screen).

In addition, there are many reputable free antiviruses on Google Play store. My favorite antiviruses are AVG, Lookout and Norton Antiviruses. You may check Google Play Store to download any of these.

Note: The best way to protect yourself from a virus attack is being proactive. For example, I don't expect you to click the links present in an unsolicited email. So, having many antiviruses on your phone may not help if you are not prudent in your actions.

Safety Precautions When Using Samsung Galaxy S9/S9 Plus on Wi-Fi

With many free Wi-Fi hotspot, it is likely that you are going to find yourself using Wi-Fi more on your phone. There are few things to keep in mind when using Wi-Fi.

1. Confirm the Network Name

Hackers sometimes set up a fake Wi-Fi network in order to tap into the information of unwitting public users. To avoid this, make sure you are sure of the name of the network you are connecting to. You may ask any trusted individual around you if you doubt the name of a network.

2. Connect to a Secured Site

Whenever you are sending a sensitive information, always make sure that the site is a secured website. You can know whether a website is a secured site or not by checking whether the *url* address of the website starts with **HTTPS.** If it starts with https, then it should be a secured site.

3. Run an Antivirus Software

As earlier mentioned, using an antivirus is very crucial in today's world. You may consider installing a genuine antivirus. There are many of them on Google Play store.

4. Get a Virtual Private Network (VPN)

It is highly important you use a virtual private network when using a public wireless network. There are both free and paid VPN providers. My favorite is **Hotspot Shield VPN.** It is available on Google Play store. They offer both free and paid versions. You may also check out other VPN apps to pick the best.

5. Avoid Automatic Connection

Make sure your Wi-Fi is off when not using it to avoid your phone automatically connecting to an open network. Turning your Wi-Fi off when not using it will also save your battery.

I am Having a Dwindling Love for my Samsung Galaxy S9/S9 Plus; What Should I Do?

It is possible that after buying Samsung Galaxy S9/S9 Plus, you realize that it performs below your expectation. It is likely that you dislike your phone because of its hardware or software issue. Generally, the hardware has to do with the design, the phone make up, the weight of the phone etc. While the software has to do with the OS and applications.

If your love for Samsung Galaxy S9/S9 Plus is reducing because of the software, there is a way out. You can take your time to look for beneficial apps to install on your device.

If your love for Samsung Galaxy S9/S9 Plus is reducing because of the hardware, then it is either you learn how to live with it (you may have to force yourself to love it), give it away or you sell it. If you are considering selling your phone or giving it away, then make sure you read the article on page 351-353.

TROUBLESHOOTING

If the touch screen responds slowly or improperly or your phone is not responding, try the following:

- Remove any protective covers (screen protector) from the touch screen.
- Ensure that your hands are clean and dry when tapping. In addition, ensure that the screen of your phone is not wet. If wet, use a soft dry towel to clean it.
- Press the power button once to lock the screen and press it again to unlock the screen and enter a PIN/password/pattern if required.
- Switch off your device and on it again.

Your phone doesn't charge

- Make sure you are using Samsung charger to charge your phone.
- If the Samsung Galaxy S9/S9 Plus does not indicate that it is charging, unplug the power adapter and then restart your device.
- Make sure you are using the USB cable that came with the Samsung Galaxy S9/S9 Plus or anyone that has similar specs.

Your device is hot to the touch

When you use applications that require more power or use applications on your device for an extended period, your phone may be a bit hot. This is normal, and it should not have much effect on its performance. You may just allow your phone to rest for some time or close some applications.

Your phone freezes or has fatal error

If your phone freezes or it is unresponsive, press and hold the Power key and the Volume Down key simultaneously until the screen goes off, then wait for it to restart automatically. Please note that you may need to press the Power key and the Volume Down key simultaneously for more than 5 seconds before the phone will restart.

Phone does not connect to Wi-Fi

Make sure you don't have limited network connectivity in that area. If your network signal is good and you still cannot connect, you may perform any of these actions.

- Make sure your Airplane Mode is off.
- Try restarting the Wi-Fi.
- Move closer to your router and scan for the available networks. If the network still does not show up, you may add the network manually.
- Restart your router and modem. Unplug the modem and router for few minutes and plug the modem in, and then the router.
- Try restarting you phone.

Phone screen color is appearing somehow

- Check if you have not mistakenly turned on blue light filter.

  To do this, go to **Settings** ⚙ > **Display** > **Blue Light Filter** > **Turn on now**.

Another Bluetooth device is not located

- Ensure Bluetooth feature is activated on your phone and the device you want to connect to.

- Ensure that your phone and the other Bluetooth device are within the maximum Bluetooth range (usually approximately 30 feet).

A connection is not established when you connect your phone to a PC using USB cable

- Ensure that the USB cable you are using is compatible with your device.

- Ensure that you have the proper drivers installed and updated on your PC.

Audio quality is poor during a call

- Ensure that the network signal is strong. When you are in an area with a weak or poor reception, you may lose reception. Try moving to another area and then try again.

Safety precautions

A. To prevent electric shock, fire, and explosion

1. Do not use damaged power cords or plugs, or loose electrical sockets.

2. Do not touch the power cord with a wet hand.

3. Do not bend or damage the power cord.

4. Do not short-circuit the charger.

5. Do not use your phone during thunderstorm.

6. Do not dispose your phone by putting it in fire.

B. Follow all safety warnings and regulations when using your device in restricted areas.

C. Comply with all safety warnings and regulations regarding mobile device usage while operating a vehicle.

D. Proper care and use of your phone

1. Do not use or store your phone in hot or cold areas. It is recommended to use your device at temperature from 5^0C to 35^0C.

2. Do not put your phone near magnetic fields.

3. Do not use camera flash close to eyes of people or pets because it can cause temporary loss of vision or damage the eyes.

4. When speaking on the phone, speak directly into the mouthpiece.

5. Avoid disturbing others when using your phone in public.

6. Keep your phone away from children because they may mistakenly damage it as it may look like a toy to them.

Just Before You Go (Please Read!)

Although I have put in tremendous effort in writing this guide,
I am confident that I have not said it all.
I have no doubt believing that I have not written everything possible
about Samsung Galaxy S9/S9 Plus.
So, I want you to do me a favor.
If you would like to know how to perform a task that is not included
in this guide, please let me know by sending me an email at
pharmibrahimguides@gmail.com. I will try as much as possible to
reply you as soon as I can.

You may also visit my author's page at
www.amazon.com/author/pharmibrahim
And please don't forget to follow me when you visit my author's
page, just click or tap on **Follow** button located below the profile
picture.

Made in the USA
Coppell, TX
18 March 2022

75203046R00207